Rethinking
Today's
Minorities

Recent Titles in Contributions in Sociology

Rethinking Today's Minorities

Edited by
Vincent N. Parrillo

CONTRIBUTIONS IN SOCIOLOGY, NUMBER 93

GREENWOOD PRESS
New York • Westport, Connecticut • London

Library of Congress Cataloging-in-Publication Data

Rethinking today's minorities / edited by Vincent N. Parrillo.
    p.   cm. — (Contributions in sociology, ISSN 0084–9278 ; no.
93)
    Includes papers from annual meetings of the Eastern Sociological
Society.
    Includes bibliographical references and index.
    ISBN 0–313–27537–8 (lib. bdg. : alk. paper)
    1. Minorities—United States—Congresses.   2. United States—
Social policy—1980– —Congresses.   I. Parrillo, Vincent N.
II. Eastern Sociological Society (U.S.)   III. Series.
E184.A1R449   1991
305.8′00973—dc20   90–40733

British Library Cataloguing in Publication Data is available.

Library of Congress Catalog Card Number: 90–40733
ISBN: 0–313–27537–8
ISSN: 0084–9278

First published in 1991

Greenwood Press, 88 Post Road West, Westport, CT 06881
An imprint of Greenwood Publishing Group, Inc.

Printed in the United States of America

The paper used in this book complies with the
Permanent Paper Standard issued by the National
Information Standards Organization (Z39.48–1984).

10 9 8 7 6 5 4 3 2 1

CONTENTS

PREFACE

This volume brings together the research and analytical commentaries of some of the nation's leading experts in the field of intergroup relations. Culled primarily from presentations at the Eastern Sociological Society annual meetings from 1987 to 1989, these chapters provide the reader with fresh insights and understandings about today's minority peoples, whether they be native-born Americans, immigrants, or refugees.

Much has changed in the United States in the 1970s and 1980s. More than 80 percent of all immigrants are now Asian or Hispanic; many of these immigrants enter with better education and job skills than previous immigrants. Thousands of Third World refugees, many with little education or job skills, seek asylum here, but only some find official welcome. American Indians and African Americans, after some socioeconomic gains, face increasing difficulty in securing the elusive "American Dream" other groups have found. In the electronic age of television and computers, new challenges and opportunities present themselves for progress, stagnation, or regression for minority rights.

Reflecting the most recent thoughts of some of the United States' most respected social scientists, these chapters are on the cutting edge of knowledge about minority groups in America. Together they sharpen our focus for policy development and social action in the last decade of the twentieth century.

PART ONE —————————————————————————

CONCEPTUAL OVERVIEW

RETHINKING TODAY'S MINORITIES

Vincent N. Parrillo

They come across the South China Sea in tiny boats, across 100 miles of ocean from Cuba in inner tubes, and brave the Rio Grande in rafts made of automobile hoods welded together. Violence, persecution, repression, and poverty may encircle their lives, but they dream of something better—of freedom. Almost 500 years old, the dream still works on the imagination like a magnet. The dream has a magic name: America.

For many who come, the passage to America is the hardest ordeal. For centuries the ocean voyage—the trial by wind and wave, hunger and sickness—was so intense an experience that few immigrants ever forgot it. Today the passage can be equally harrowing. Almost any waiter in a Vietnamese restaurant in Houston, Texas, or Orange County, California, has a tale of walking across Cambodia or fleeing Vietnam by boat, of attacks by ruthless Thai pirates, and of long months in a refugee camp. The Cambodians have their holocaust, the Haitians their small boats, the Mexicans their encounters with the feared *La Migra*, the border patrol.

But no danger seems too great and no obstacle too large to stop those who are determined to come. First the name—Amer-

This chapter was originally presented at the Eastern Sociological Society annual meeting, Boston, May 1, 1987.

ica—begins to circulate in towns and villages, then the idea takes hold, and the flood begins. Millions of people forsake the lands of their ancestors, give up old traditions and old dreams to pursue new dreams and new traditions. For most of us, America is a gift long since given; for each new arrival, it is fresh and dynamic and not to be squandered. Each new immigrant re-creates the American dream.

Today we are living in a reawakening of the immigrant experience. Not since the first decade of the twentieth century have so many new immigrants become Americans. Over 5 million legal immigrants entered the United States in the 1980s, with perhaps millions more entering illegally. New ethnic neighborhoods are transforming U.S. cities. New faces are turning up in shops and factories. New languages buzz in the schools. This bubbling stew may seem strange to some, but until immigration was all but cut off in 1924, it was once the normal condition of America.

Yet, even though the flow of immigrants in this decade will be among the largest in history, the annual number of immigrants hovers around only 0.2 percent of the total population; before 1924 the figure was routinely more than 1 percent (U.S. Immigration and Naturalization Service, 1990). The U.S. foreign-born population in 1980 was less than half of what it was in 1910. In Boston in 1885 almost 70 percent of the population was foreign-born. Two-thirds to three-fourths of the population of most of the major cities east of the Mississippi were foreign-born at the turn of the century. Today even Los Angeles—where almost a third of the population is foreign-born—does not begin to approach these figures (Siegel, 1982).

Today we are living through the third major period of immigration in U.S. history. The first period, 1820–1860, brought the United States 5 million immigrants, mostly Irish and German. The second period, 1880–1920, saw 23 million immigrants arrive, mostly from southern, central, and eastern Europe. In the third wave, since 1965, more than 10 million newcomers have entered the country, most of them Asians or Latinos. Of the more than 500,000 legal immigrants admitted to the United States each year between 1981 and 1989, 48 percent were from Asia and 35 percent from Latin America. Immigration from Europe, historically the principal source of newcomers, fell to 11 percent (U.S. Immigration and Naturalization Service, 1990). South Korea alone sends more than England, West Germany, Ireland, and Italy put together—the nations that for the past 650 years furnished the great majority of immigrants to America.

In the previous two major immigration periods, most of the immigrants were of low socioeconomic status, following a chain migration pattern, clustering in ethnic enclaves, and re-creating in miniature the world they left behind. Thus insulated against a strange and often insensitive outside world, many past immigrants utilized their ethnic subcommunity as a decompression chamber before entrance into the larger society. With their parallel social institutions, endogamous marriages, and subcultural lifestyles, these immigrants slowly became acculturated, and, at some point one or more generations later, most usually joined the mainstream of American society.

Clearly, some of today's immigrants still follow that pattern. In many cities, for instance, one can find poor or working-class Hispanic neighborhoods that are not only filled with recent arrivals but the newcomers concentrated in clusters of, say, Ecuadorians, Colombians, or Peruvians. Like the central and eastern European immigrants before them, they discover that native-born Americans usually ignore their many cultural and nationalistic differences, instead lumping them all together in the single category of "Hispanic." Indeed, the annual reports of many government agencies, once past the classification of Cuban, Mexican, and Puerto Rican, tend to place the remaining Latino peoples into the category "other, Spanish," even when this group totals as high as 36.2 percent (Parrillo, 1990: 413).

Similarly, many of the poor or working-class immigrants are nonwesterners clustered together in recognizable ethnic neighborhoods. For example, large concentrations of Filipinos can be found in Los Angeles and Stockton, California; Koreans in Los Angeles, Chicago, and New York; and Chinese in San Francisco and New York.

Additionally, small clusters of refugees also exist in many parts of the country, such as Hmong from Laos in Seattle; Haitians in Dade County, Florida; and Vietnamese in New Orleans and Denver. Although many of the nonwestern refugees face problems of mental stress and severe adjustment from a preliterate, agrarian past life into a postindustrial America, their acculturation and adjustment patterns nonetheless also are reminiscent of past immigrant patterns.

Whether immigrant or refugee, Hispanic or nonwesterner, the newcomers are struggling to gain a foothold in their adopted land and to establish a better life for their children and themselves. In terms of their goals and motivation, residential settlement, evolution of ethnic subcommunities, and acculturation, such immigrants provide a replication of sociohistorical patterns.

We even find continuing associations between ethnicity and occupation. A few examples are Filipino nurses, Vietnamese restaurant operators, Indian newsstand dealers, and Korean grocers. Falling into the marginality patterns discussed by Everett Stonequist (1937) and Georg Simmel (1937), immigrants such as these still migrate and find their niche in society. They fill roles in the economy that the native-born do not see or want, and they succeed in them. The President's Council of Economic Advisers has argued that immigrants have a net positive effect on the economy in general. In 1985 the Rand Corporation concluded that overall, Mexican immigration has probably been an economic asset to California.

Yet a large proportion of today's immigrants no longer fit nicely into the time-honored framework for analyzing immigration and assimilation. When U.S. immigration laws changed in 1965, the occupational preference schedule gave a higher priority to those with educational levels and job skills enabling them to find more easily their niche in postindustrial America. Consequently, many of today's immigrants, particularly nonwesterners, enter the United States more literate and with marketable skills. They can get professional and salaried jobs without first having to play a subservient role in the economy. They need not yield to pressures to conform to the American way of life in order to gain middle-class respectability. Their income is high enough to enable them to enjoy the lifestyle they want, and they are thus free to continue their own cultural behavior patterns. Some Americanization will undoubtedly occur, but these immigrants do not have to make substantial adaptations in order to make it in American society.

Therefore, there is presently a large-scale influx of foreigners able to enter the U.S. economic mainstream but who remain physical, cognitive, and behavioral minorities. The nonwestern immigrants are physical minorities in that they differ in appearance from archetypes or social norms. They are cognitive minorities, a term coined by Peter Berger (1967), in that they differ in political, religious, or social doctrines from social norms. They are behavioral minorities in that they differ in their patterns of social conduct from those of the host society (Newman, 1973: 34–38).

Because they are still part of two worlds—that of their particular group and that of the larger society—immigrants live in a world of what Alfred Schutz (1945) called "multiple realities." Individuals therefore often confront role choices involving differing values, perception, and behaviors. Faced with a conflicting role choice, individuals can choose to adapt, resist, or withdraw from the host society's definition. How are today's affluent but unassimilated immigrants likely to act? Would their responses be similar to or different from those of earlier but less affluent immigrants?

What sociologists need to examine is how valid are theoretical orientations and conceptual models when applied to those first-generation Americans whose possession of rewards and resources far surpass those of past immigrants but whose minority visibility and social isolation is comparable to previous immigrants. What exactly are we seeing? Do analytical frameworks still work? Or must an entirely new theoretical model be created? For example, how relevant is social conflict theory for a minority group mostly comprised of middle-class immigrants not experiencing exploitation, yet possessing resources and access to societal institutions and nevertheless socially segregated? How relevant is Stonequist's concept (1937) of marginal man, which assumes secluded living in ethnic enclaves, for recent newcomers whose reference group remains their own although they live and work with native-born Americans and enjoy a comfortable lifestyle?

Of course, no single theory has ever satisfactorily served to explain all immigrant experiences. The sociological study of intergroup relations has generated several different and often conflicting theoretical approaches. There exist macrosocial and microsocial perspectives, and, under each of these, numerous middle-range theories can be found. The result has been numerous studies with conflicting themes about the nature of intergroup relationships in the United States.

Despite the many theoretical viewpoints, a considerable body of sociological knowledge has evolved. Hundreds of studies of all kinds of ethnic enclaves have been conducted. We know, for example, a great deal about Jewish neighborhoods, Little Italies, Poletowns, Greektowns, Little Hungaries, Russiantowns, Germantowns, and Dublin Districts. We're beginning to learn more about Little Havanas, Little Haitis, Little Manilas, Little Saigons, and Koreatowns too.

Evolving out of this body of knowledge, and indeed predating some of the studies, have been the contributions of many theorists. Several of them have attempted to explain the multiple pattern possibilities of minority adaptation. The central theme of Milton Gordon's seminal work, *Assimilation in American Life* (1964), is that assimilation is not a single social process but a number of different subprocesses or dimensions. Most important, Gordon maintained, were cultural and structural assimilation. Earlier, Louis Wirth (1945) identified four distinct approaches minority groups could take to the larger society: pluralism, assimilation, secession, and militancy. For Wirth and many others, situational variables play a significant role in determining a minority group's response to society.

Clearly, situational variables play a large role in understanding the adjustment to American life by today's Asian and Hispanic immigrants. The educational, occupational, and socioeconomic diversity existing among today's immigrants makes that point rather evident. Are existing theories still valid in their application to today's immigrants? Before we can answer this question, we must identify just how today's immigrants differ from past immigrants in their adaptation patterns.

Because many of today's immigrants are trained professionals or skilled technicians, their income enables them to settle in middle-class urban or suburban neighborhoods, not in decaying sections of cities as did earlier European immigrants. Further, they seldom locate next to one another in adjacent dwellings, thereby preventing the establishment of recognizable ethnic territorial neighborhoods. Theirs is an interactional community rather than a territorial one. Ethnic solidarity is maintained through a cosmopolitan network of communication and life cycle rituals (births, graduations, weddings, deaths). Their sense of community is also maintained by homeland concerns, political activism, or limited social situations (work, school, nearby families).

The dispersed settlement pattern found among today's middle-class immigrants is not confined to that social strata alone. Except for most Chinese, Korean, and Filipino newcomers, other working-class nonwestern immigrants tend to follow the same settlement and interaction patterns (Agocs, 1981; Aswad, 1974; Parrillo, 1983). Vincent Parrillo's study (1983) of almost 6,000 working-class Arab immigrants living in the Paterson, New Jersey, metropolitan area revealed a similar choice. Instead of settling in historic inner-city areas or zones of transition, Arab immigrants tend to reside on the edge of cities instead, in a loose clustering, often living several doors or blocks away from another Arab. Their houses of worship range from two to five miles distance from their residence. They work mostly with outgroup members but rarely socialize with anyone outside their ethnic group. They participate in all American social institutions except religious ones, and meaningful primary relationships exist within the sphere of their subcultural world.

A Sikh temple, a mosque, a Melkite Catholic church, or a Korean Christian church offers an obvious visual clue to the presence of an ethnic group, but its members do not necessarily live nearby any more than they are to be found clustered together in ethnic neighborhoods. Today's affluent immigrants often travel several miles in their cars to attend their ethnic house of worship. For them, religion is important in maintaining an ethnic identity in pluralistic America, a pattern reminiscent of earlier European immigrants. One study, for example, of the role of Korean churches in the ethnic community of Chicago, where over 50,000 Koreans live, found church affiliation was 57 percent compared to 12 percent in Korea (Kim, Hurh, and Kim, 1979).

This heightened interest in church membership and frequent attendance at worship services are common among new immigrant groups seeking a communal bond in their ethnic identity.

Social distance ranking, a measurement device created by Emory Bogardus in 1926, is one means of identifying the social integration of various groups. Since then it has been repeatedly used to measure the degree of social closeness or distance personally acceptable with members of a particular outgroup (Bogardus, 1968). Most recent applications of this research tool still find near-bottom social distance rankings for Koreans and other nonwesterners, despite their economic stability (Hurh, 1977: 68).

Further evidence of economic mainstreaming but continuing social segregation of many of today's immigrants is emerging from numerous field research studies (Parrillo, 1984; Elkholy, 1981; Ansari, 1988). What appears to be emerging among many first-generation immigrants today is a social segregation pattern comparable to one that researchers in the late 1950s and early 1960s found among second- and third-generation Jewish Americans living in the suburbs. Gerhard Lenski (1961) in Detroit, John P. Dean (1955) in Elmira, New York, Herbert J. Gans (1958) in Park Forest, Illinois, and Albert Gordon (1956) all reported relative isolation of Jews in evening or weekend social gatherings with non-Jewish friends. Daytime social activities involved the entire neighborhoods, but, as one housewife remarked, "At five o'clock a curtain comes down between us" (Gans, 1958).

Although the situation has changed somewhat for American Jews since then, today's immigrants experience much the same thing. They work side by side with native-born Americans in the workplace, interacting with one another as white-collar colleagues. However, few meaningful primary relationships evolve between the two group members, and social interactions outside the workplace are rare. Not completely by choice, today's immigrants tend to live and work in mixed group settings but interact in meaningful primary relationships with members of their own religio-ethnic group.

The concept of marginality doesn't quite fit today's middle-class immigrants. Granted, they are somewhat caught between two worlds, their values and cultural patterns occasionally in conflict with those of the host society. On the other hand, they are at ease within their own group, which remains their reference group. Further, they do not attempt to enter the mainstream because they already have done so in most respects. However, they are a study in contrasts. They live in interactional not territorial communities. They are structurally assimilated into most societal institutions but remain socially segregated. They blend into the American workplace yet retain their ethnic identity outside it. They are part of the economic mainstream but encourage endogamy. They remain visibly distinct but encounter little prejudice or discrimination.

A good term to describe their dual existence in the United States might be "Alien Americans." They are fully American in their economic mainstreaming, residential settlement patterns, affluent lifestyle, and participation in societal institutions. Nevertheless, they remain aliens, unknown strangers, in the social world about them, even in their own neighborhoods. Generally isolated, except on rare occasions, from informal social contact with others outside their nationality group, the newcomers by necessity interact with compatriots, remaining a generalized entity in American minds. This social segregation appears to result more from an attraction toward similarly perceived others than overt avoidance. Nonetheless, these immigrants live a dual existence, not a marginal one.

Having fine-tuned the conceptual model of today's immigrants, we must ask the question: Are existing theories adequate to explain these seemingly contrasting patterns? We would suggest that they are, as long as the foregoing is considered. Only then will accurate analysis be possible.

The order theories of assimilation and pluralism are broad enough to encompass today's diverse immigrants. Whether examining skilled or unskilled, poor or affluent, immigrants or refugees, the functionalist or consensus theorists can study them as temporary dysfunctions within the inherent order of American society. Their emphasis can continue to be upon a linear adjustment process toward eventual group combination or the retention by ethnic groups of some form of social pluralism. Milton Gordon's identification of the assimilation process as both a matter of degree and of various subprocesses can certainly apply. Pluralists, whether promoting the existence of cultural pluralism as an ongoing reality in American history or supporting Nathan Glazer and Daniel Moynihan's (1970) modified form of hyphenated Americans maintaining that social identity yet integrated within the larger American society, can also cite much evidence to support their positions.

Similarly, conflict theory has much grist for its mill. Most obvious are the modern sweatshops exploiting both legal and illegal aliens, and the flare-ups of violence such as that directed against Vietnamerican shrimp fishermen along the Texas Gulf Coast. As for minority groups simultaneously experiencing both reward parity and social segregation, conflict theorists do have a foundation upon which to base their analysis. William Newman (1973: 170–174), for example, observed that parity of social resources, coupled with social segregation, is evidence of the minority group's (1) desire for disengagement, (2) rejection of some segment of the values and norms of the host society, and (3) ability to impose its own self-definition of its distinctiveness as strongly subcultural. With their focus upon tensions, power struggles, competition for limited resources, and change, conflict theorists will continue to find a fertile field in the current wave of immigration.

Third, interactionists will have no difficulty analyzing current intergroup relations. All their concerns about the presence or absence of shared histories, understandings, and interpretations remain pertinent. Equally valid are emphases upon visual and verbal clues, categorizing, communication, and symbolic interaction. The contrasts in background and acculturation patterns between past and present immigrants are unimportant to interactionist theorists. What matters are the personal interaction patterns in everyday life today, and they can be examined without reliance on a conceptual model.

Regardless of one's theoretical orientation, two observations hold true. First, the present migration patterns are creating in the United States a land of greater racial and cultural diversity then ever before. Just as Irish Catholics and German Jews changed the complexion of nineteenth-century America, and southern, central, and eastern Europeans altered the face of America by the early twentieth century, so too is the present

Asian and Hispanic influx varying the population composition still further. Second, today's immigrants fit no single mold, either in their backgrounds or in their way of adjusting to American life. If we ignore the variations among the multiple acculturation models, we may well thwart any accurate analysis and interpretation about what we see.

REFERENCES

Agocs, Carol. "Ethnic Settlement in a Metropolitan Area: A Typology of Communities," *Ethnicity*, 8 (1981), 127–148.

Ansari, Maboud. *The Iranians in the United States*. New York: Associated Faculty Press, 1988.

Aswad, B. *Arabic Speaking Communities in American Cities*. New York: Center for Migration Studies, 1974.

Berger, Peter L. *The Sacred Canopy: Elements of a Sociological Theory of Religion*. New York: Doubleday, 1967.

Bogardus, Emory M. "Comparing Racial Distance in Ethiopia, South Africa, and United States," *Sociology and Social Research*, 52 (1968), 149–156.

Dean, John P. "Patterns of Socialization and Association Between Jews and Non-Jews," *Jewish Social Studies*, 17 (July 1955), 252–254.

Elkholy, Abdo A. "The Arab American Family," in Charles H. Mindel and Robert W. Habenstein (eds.), *Ethnic Families in America*, 2d ed. New York: Elsevier, 1981.

Gans, Herbert J. "The Origin and Growth of a Jewish Community in the Suburbs: A Study of the Jews of Park Forest," in Marshall Sklare (ed.), *The Jews: Social Patterns of an American Group*. Glencoe, IL: Free Press, 1958.

Glazer, Nathan, and Daniel P. Moynihan. *Beyond the Melting Pot*, 2d ed. Cambridge, MA: MIT Press, 1970.

Gordon, Albert I. *Jews in Suburbia*. Boston: Beacon Press, 1956.

Gordon, Milton M. *Assimilation in American Life*. New York: Oxford University Press, 1964.

Hurh, Won Moo. "Comparative Study of Korean Immigrants in the United States: A Typology," *Korean Christian Journal*, 2 (Spring 1977), 73–85.

Kim, Hei Chu, Won Moo Hurh, and Kwang Chung Kim. "Ethnic Roles of the Korean Church in the Chicago Area." Paper presented at the annual meeting of the Korean Christian Scholars Association, Boston, June 1979.

Lenski, Gerhard. *The Religious Factor*. New York: Doubleday, 1961.

Newman, William M. *American Pluralism: A Study of Minority Groups and Social Theory.* New York: Harper & Row, 1973.

Parrillo, Vincent N. "Arab American Immigrant Communities: Diversity and Parallel." Paper presented at annual meetings of Eastern Sociological Society, Baltimore, March 1983.

———. "Arab American Residential Segregation: Differences in Patterns." Paper presented at annual meetings of Eastern Sociological Society, Boston, March 1984.

———. *Strangers to These Shores,* 3d ed. New York: Macmillan, 1990.

Schutz, Alfred. "The Stranger," *American Sociological Review,* 69 (May 1944), 499–507.

———. "On Multiple Realities," *Philosophy and Phenomenological Research,* 5 (June 1945), 533–576.

Siegel, Barry. "Here We Come Again," *Los Angeles Times,* December 12, 1982, p. 1.

Simmel, Georg. "The Stranger," in Kurt H. Wolff (ed.), *The Sociology of Georg Simmel.* New York: Scribner, 1937.

Stonequist, Everett V. *The Marginal Man.* New York: Scribner, 1937.

U.S. Immigration and Naturalization Service. *Annual Report.* Washington, DC: U.S. Government Printing Office, 1990.

Wirth, Louis. "The Problem of Minority Groups," in Ralph Linton (ed.), *The Science of Man in the World Crisis.* New York: Columbia University Press, 1945.

World Development Forum. *The Hunger Project,* vol. 5, no. 2, January 31, 1987.

THE NEW ETHNICS: FAMILIAR STRAINS IN DIFFERENT SETTINGS

Vincent N. Parrillo

Since 1980, the United States has experienced the biggest flow of immigrants in the memory of almost any living American. This nation has recently absorbed twice as many immigrants as the rest of the countries in the world combined. Although the ceiling on U.S. immigration is under 500,000 annually, immediate relatives of U.S. citizens are exempt from that cap, and the actual legal immigration has averaged 567,000 a year in the 1980s (U.S. Immigration and Naturalization Service [INS], 1990.

In the 1970s, the United States received almost 4.5 million legal immigrants and admitted over 5 million immigrants between 1981 and 1989 (INS, 1990). If this trend continues, and all indicators suggest that it will, this immigration period may surpass the heaviest one this far in American history, the period between 1880 and 1920, when 23 million newcomers entered the United States.

Only one in ten immigrants now comes from Europe. About 3 percent come from Africa, triple the rate in the 1960s. Currently, more than 30 percent of the annual immigrants are from Latin America, and almost half are Asian (INS, 1990). In the words of Ben Wattenberg, quoted in *The Newest Americans*—which is a fine report of the American Jewish Committee's Task

A revised version of this chapter was presented at the Eastern Sociological Society annual meeting, Philadelphia, March 11, 1988.

Force on the Acculturation of Immigrants to American Life—the U.S. is becoming the "first universal nation" (Task Force on the Acculturation of Immigrants to American Life, 1987).

Obviously, these immigration patterns are changing the composition of the American population. Between April 1, 1980, and July 1, 1986, the nonwhite, nonblack category of "other races" increased 45 percent to total 7.5 million. "Other races" consists mainly of Asians, American Indians, Alaskan natives, and Pacific Islanders. In the same period the white population grew 4.9 percent and the black population grew 9.8 percent (U.S. Bureau of the Census, 1987).

Trend extrapolation of birth and migration patterns suggests the extent of our changing population. Asian Americans, who numbered approximately 3.5 million in 1980, will almost triple in number to about 10 million by the turn of the century (Bouvier and Agresta, 1987). Hispanic Americans, numbering over 14.6 million in 1980, may total as many as 31.2 million by the year 2000 (U.S. Bureau of the Census, 1987). Clearly, today's immigrants are becoming a more and more visible presence, just as southern, central, and eastern Europeans were in the early twentieth century.

But demography is only one component of the new immigration wave. Analysis of intergroup relations, majority/minority interaction patterns, and variation in resettlement and acculturation patterns all provide other avenues for sociological inquiry to aid our understanding of what is actually happening in this "nation of immigrants." While it is impossible within the parameters of this chapter to describe fully all the diverse groups and all the varied experiences, let us concentrate upon some of the major patterns and common touchstones that many of today's immigrants share. Our emphasis here shall be that, despite different national origins and cultures, and despite different structural conditions in American society, these patterns are echoes of the past. Unfortunately, not all these patterns are positive ones.

XENOPHOBIC FEARS

Peppered throughout U.S. history are numerous examples of expressed fears about threats to the country by the presence of a large, foreign-born population. The sentiments expressed, for example, in 1798 by William Smith Shaw, the young nephew of President John Adams, are remarkably similar to those heard today. Writing to First Lady Abigail Adams, Shaw wrote, "The grand cause of our present difficulties may be traced . . . to so many hordes of Foreigners imigrating [sic] to America. . . . Let us no longer pray that America may become an asylum to all nations" (*Adams Papers*).

Antiimmigration cartoons have often effectively depicted deep-seated fears among native-born Americans about "waves" and "hordes" of "un-American types" inundating the United States. The following are just four examples of these cartoons against open immigration that appeared over a ninety-year period.

1. In a June 22, 1893, issue of *Life*, E. M. Ashe illustrated a sleeping Uncle Sam lethargically putting up his feet in his garden while a stream of foreign rats invaded it. The rats' faces were stereotypical depictions of Jews, Russians, Italians, Greeks, and other southern and central Europeans. The caption read, "How long will it be before the rats own the garden and the man gets out?"

2. In February 1921, several months before passage of a restrictive immigration law, the *Los Angeles Times* ran a cartoon by Gale with the caption, "Spoiling the broth!" A huge barrel labeled "Europe and Asia's Teeming Millions" was tilted and pouring a "flood of immigration" into a smaller, symbolic melting pot overflowing with "unassimilated aliens" while Uncle Sam stood, with his back turned, reading a newspaper about the business outlook.

3. The January 12, 1922, issue of *Life* carried a cartoon by J. M. Flagg, showing foreign-born Americans crowding around and staring at a timid WASP (white Anglo-Saxon Protestant) male. A sideshow barker stood next to him pointing to a sign reading, "The Last Yankee in Captivity." Underneath the cartoon appeared this limerick:

   In nineteen seventy-five
   Crowds swarmed like bees 'round a hive
   To see in a tent
   An American gent—
   The very last Yankee alive.

4. In June 1984, two years before passage of immigration reform legislation, Jim Morin drew for the *Miami Herald* a cartoon showing a

cresting tidal wave of humanity about to crash upon the shoreline
and over the head of one symbolic American holding a stop sign;
his suit was labeled Simpson-Mazzoli, the name of the proposed bill
before Congress. Both *Newsweek* and *Time* reprinted the cartoon in
their July 2, 1984, issues, thereby extending this antiimmigration
message to a national audience.

Morin's 1984 cartoon is as reminiscent of past fears as is the
1987 statement of Cornell economist Vernon M. Briggs, Jr.: "We
simply can't let sentiment and reverence for the Statue of Liberty
guide our immigration policies in the 1990s as they did in the
1890s" (Briggs, 1987). Briggs believes that less than 5 percent of
the newcomers have the skills and education in demand by U.S.
employers, thereby creating a heavy drain on the nation's resources. His urging for stronger entry restrictions reminds us of
others who have sought to shut our doors to immigrants and
refugees, or at least close the doors part way.

Similarly, when *U.S. News & World Report* headlined a six-
page feature article "The Great American Immigration Nightmare" (Kelly, 1981), or when a daily metropolitan newspaper
headlined a lifestyle page feature "Can Lady Liberty Ever Say
No?" (Schulman, 1974), we find further evidence of the expression of immigration fears.

How real are such fears? Speaking purely from a quantitative
viewpoint, the impact of slightly over 5 million immigrants in
the 1980s upon a population of 240 million people (a 2.5 percent
immigration rate) is certainly less than the 10.4 percent immigration rate for the 8.8 million who arrived between 1901 and
1910 in a country then totaling 92 million people (INS, 1990).
Surely, the 1.7 million immigrants arriving in the peak year 1907,
when the total population numbered about 87 million, was more
significant than the average 567,000 arriving yearly in the 1980s.

CHAIN MIGRATION

One easily recognizable parallel between past and present
immigrants lies in their networks of migration. The vanguard
of a sending country's emigrants has regularly written back
home to friends and relatives, informing them of where to live

and find work in the United States. Though separated by wide oceans, those who followed left their homelands knowing exactly where they wanted to go and how to get there.

Thousands of Poles were brought from Gdansk to Polish Hill in Pittsburg by aunts, uncles, brothers, and sisters who sent them passage money and instructions of what to bring and where to make steamship and railroad connections. By 1915, as a result of such patterns, investigators could find heavy clusters of families in city neighborhoods. About three-fourths of the Italians and one-half of the Jews who owned property in Providence, Rhode Island, lived in a building with kin at the same address. . . . Chicanos followed each other along railroad lines into Los Angeles and from there throughout southern California. (Bodnar, 1985: 57)

Indeed, historian John Bodnar reminds us that relatives and friends were often responsible for movement to second and third locations in America when employment became slack in areas of first settlement. Thus, Italians from southern Illinois moved to the Italian "hill" in St. Louis when coal mining operations were reduced in the 1920s, and Slavs from mines in western Pennsylvania and northern Michigan moved to Detroit's expanding car industry in the same decade (Bodnar, 1985: 58).

Similar chain migration patterns can be found among the newest Americans. One need only look, for example, at the clusters of Egyptian Coptic Christians in Jersey City; Iranians in Fairfax County, Virginia; Arabs in the Detroit metropolitan area; Filipinos in Stockton, California; the Koreatowns and various Hispanic neighborhoods flourishing in many cities; and the myriad of other ethnic communities taking root in the land. The second and third locations become evident by noting the intended residence of new arrivals joining relatives and compatriots at interior sites. For example, significant numbers of Vietnamese are settling in Houston, thousands of Asian Indians are choosing Chicago, and Boston is becoming the selection of Chinese, the latter group being the more numerous arrivals there than most other ethnic groups (INS, 1987).

FAMILY ECONOMY

As was the case with past immigrants, many of the newest Americans come from a world in which the family is the central focus. Despite differences in religion, cultural background, and positioning within the economy, for most immigrant families in initial decades of settlement, familial and communal networks abound. Most especially, members of nearly all groups receive intense socialization and reinforcement into the values of family loyalty, cooperation, and sharing.

By working together, pooling limited resources and muting individual inclinations, families attempted to assemble the resources sufficient for economic survival and, occasionally, for an improvement in their standard of living. But the first goal was always most immediate: cooperate and survive. (Bodnar, 1985: 72)

Abundant evidence exists of the cooperative family work efforts among today's immigrants. The Hmong from Laos have settled on Minnesota farms, the Korean green grocers in most major cities, the Mexicans living in Chicago in the old Czech-Polish neighborhood called Pilsan just south of the Loop, and the Asian Indian "ma-and-pa" retail stores in countless urban and suburban settings are but a few examples.

Not all immigrant families function alike, and varying paths of education, occupation, and mobility exist among present-day immigrant families. Nevertheless, one can discern strong patterns of the family economy through which the newcomers order their lives, much like the early-twentieth-century Japanese farmers in California, Italian dye shop workers in New Jersey, Jewish garment workers in New York, and Portuguese fishermen in New England.

POLITICAL ACTIVITY

Today's immigrants appear to be repeating a past pattern of three general and overlapping phases of political action (Parrillo, 1982). The earliest is the alien phase, when the political locus remains in the nation of origin. As a form of decompression chamber in the transition from their native land to their adopted land, the immigrants in this phase re-create, in miniature, the land they left behind, including the political institutions. As a result, the organizations and social institutions they develop within the ethnic community reflect the continuance of cultural traditions, with political attention focused on the homeland.

Second is the reactionary phase, where societal hostility toward the group culminates in the use of political power against them in the form of legislative actions and judicial rulings. Usually, one response of the ethnic group is to form political organizations—not necessarily to vote, since many are not yet citizens, but to protect their interests and to fight discrimination directed against them.

The final phase, acceptance, finds greater receptivity to the group by American society, as evidenced usually by an end to overt discrimination and the ethnic group displaying a greater degree of cultural and structural assimilation.

LANGUAGE

Immigrants' retention of their native language and slowness in learning English has been a bone of contention since colonial times. The Dutch in New York did not even introduce English into their schools until 1774, a full 110 years after Britain took control of the former Dutch colony, New Netherland (Koningsberger, 1968: 20). George Washington wrote a letter to John Adams lamenting the fact that immigrants settle together and retain their language (Parrillo, 1990: 125). Ben Franklin complained in 1750 that, because there were now so many Germans with a meager knowledge of English concentrated in the colony of Pennsylvania, interpreters were necessary. "I suppose in a few years," he complained, "they will also be necessary in the Assembly, to tell one-half of our legislators what the other half say" (Parrillo, 1990: 142).

The language new Americans speak in their adopted land remains today a controversial and sensitive issue. Contrary to nativist fears, almost all Asian and Hispanic immigrants want to acquire English in order to succeed. English, however, is a difficult language to master, and one intent of bilingual education is to aid in that language acquisition. Hostile reactions to bilingual education often expand into broader fears. For instance, consider this excerpt from an editorial appearing in the March 31, 1986, issue of *U.S. News & World Report*:

> Today, the melting pot isn't working as it used to, and the very idea is under attack. The unifying force of English is being eroded. In the old days, immigrants were taught English in the public schools. Today, they are taught in Spanish, Chinese, Japanese, Arabic, and 107 other languages funded by 139 million federal dollars.
>
> Do we know what we are doing? (Evans, 1986)

For many Americans English-speaking schools provide the heat for the melting pot. Anything else, they feel, is counterproductive because it reduces assimilation and societal cohesiveness. Such sentiments, in general terms, are new versions of past expressions of immigration fears.

Duality of language, even if temporary, is problematic in other ways besides schooling. In the modest, mostly white, middle-class Olney neighborhood of north-central Philadelphia, Koreans have become a new, dynamic presence. When, with city government approval, the Koreans affixed street signs in their language to the English signs in July 1986, the residents were outraged. Quickly calling a meeting, they voted 200 to 1 to force the removal of the Korean signs by legal means. Before legal action could be taken, however, vandals destroyed twenty-five of the signs and mangled or spray-painted the rest (Stevens, 1986).

Elsewhere in the land, a dozen states, including California (which has one of the largest Asian and Hispanic populations in the nation), have passed legislation making English the official language of the state. Another twenty-five to thirty states are considering similar bills. These bills are mostly symbolic, having little practical effect, since federal law still mandates bilingual programs in our schools. Some ethnic leaders view such legislation as divisive, while others see it as no threat, as merely a clarification to newcomers of the primacy of English and its providing greater opportunities for advancement with better communication skills. Whatever the purpose or outcome, these state laws remind us of other past instances when the dominant group has used legislative control to deal with perceived threats from immigrant and/or minority peoples.

RELIGION

Following the arrival of millions of Catholics and Jews during the great migration period of 1880–1920, the construction of their many churches, convents, synagogues, and schools provided ample evidence of a changing American society. For some, these new structures further heightened nativist suspicions and fears.

Today almost 2,000 eastern and middle-eastern temples and mosques exist in the United States (U.S. Bureau of the Census, 1987). In many cases, they have smoothly blended into their community, but in other instances resistance has been significant. An example of this is Independence, a Warren County farm community in northwestern New Jersey. There a 1,500-family Hindu immigrant group from Flushing, New York, comprised mostly of well-educated professionals, purchased a 162-acre former dairy farm. They then announced an ambitious 10-year plan to build a marble temple, a 200-student school, dormitories, a community center, a health clinic, and 30 single-family homes. The scale of this development sparked a backlash as a coalition of several hundred local homeowners formed to oppose the plan and succeeded in having the township committee twice veto it. Helping fan fears was a videotape circulated by residents of Independence comparing Hinduism to Nazism. Arguing that preserving the community's size and character, not racial prejudice, was their motivation, the townspeople braced themselves for a legal battle over the matter. This issue of a rural town's right to preserve its smallness (population 3,000) and an immigrant group's right to set down its ethnic and religious roots will be resolved in the courts (Kelly, 1986). Not all intergroup disputes are settled peacefully, however.

VIOLENCE

In Brooklyn's Gravesend section, a predominantly middle-class Italian and Jewish section, about 3,000 flyers were distributed in fall 1987 saying Chinese and Koreans were using money from drug sales and Reverend Sung Myung Moon's Unification Church to buy property and that no one in the area should sell their homes to Asians. Accusations of Asians taking over neighborhoods is also heard in poor black communities, with violence sometimes being encouraged. In Philadelphia in December 1986, a popular black disc jockey reportedly said on the air that Koreans "suck our blood" and that blacks should "use kerosene" to stop them. Protests from Korean and Jewish groups led to a public apology by the radio station (United Press International, 1987).

One tragic outcome of nativist concerns escalating into xenophobic fears is the subsequent violent outbreaks they often trigger against immigrant minorities. Even the casual student of American minority relations can recall numerous past instances of such incidents. Unfortunately, one can also find present-day illustrations. Individually, they may seem to be local, isolated occurrences. Collectively, however, they suggest a recurring pattern of racial and antiforeign violence.

Consider just a few examples from the mid–1980s:

1. baseball-bat slayings of a Chinese man in Detroit and an Asian Indian in Jersey City;

2. the baseball-bat beating of a Laotian in Philadelphia and of another Asian Indian in Jersey City;

3. dozens of firebombings of Korean stores in Harlem, Philadelphia, and Washington, DC;

4. beating of Vietnamese fishermen and the torching of their boats in Texas and California;

5. tire slashings, windshield smashings, and attempted porch firebombings against Cambodians in Revere, Massachusetts; and

6. the drowning murder of a 13-year-old Cambodian boy in Lowell, Massachusetts, by an 11-year-old white who made a racial remark and pushed the Cambodian youngster into a canal. (United Press International, November 8, 1987)

The incidents of violence are now so numerous that the U.S. Commission on Civil Rights concluded in a 1986 report that violence against Asians is a national problem, with a 62 percent yearly increase occurring in anti-Asian incidents (Wong, 1986).

CONCLUSION

These violent episodes, disturbing in themselves but alarming in their frequent incidence, suggest a growing xenophobic violent reaction pattern to racially and culturally distinct newcomers, not unlike the past. The concept of the United States becoming a "universal nation," more culturally pluralistic and multiracial than ever before, has created familiar strains within the nation. The responses witnessed today to the large influx of Asian and Hispanic immigrants in many ways echo those responses to Irish Catholics and German Jews in the mid-nineteenth century and to southern, central, and eastern European immigrants in the early twentieth century. Social scientists need to examine this social phenomenon more fully. We live in the midst of profound demographic changes and their subsequent ripple effects. A vast pool of exciting research opportunities presents itself. Let us plunge in.

REFERENCES

Adams Papers, vol. 8, no. 48, Massachusetts Historical Society, May 20, 1798.

Bodnar, John. *The Transplanted*. Bloomington: Indiana University Press, 1985.

Bouvier, Leon F., and Anthony J. Agresta. "The Future Asian Population of the United States," in James T. Fawcett and Benjamin V. Carino (eds.), *Pacific Bridges: The New Immigration from Asia and the Pacific Islands*. Staten Island, NY: Center for Migration Studies, 1987.

Briggs, Vernon M., Jr. "The Growth and Composition of the U.S. Labor Force," *Science*, 238 (October 9, 1987), 176–180.

"But Can It Work?" *Time*, July 2, 1984, pp. 12–14.

Evans, Harold. "Melting Pot—or Salad Bowl," *U.S. News & World Report*, March 31, 1986, p. 76.

"Immigration: Reform at Last," *Newsweek*, July 2, 1984, p. 24.

Kelly, Michael. "A Test of Independence," *Sunday Record*, June 1, 1986, p. A1.

Kelly, Orr. "The Great American Immigration Nightmare," *U.S. News & World Report*, June 22, 1981, pp. 27–31.

Koningsberger, Hans. *Holland and the United States*. New York: Netherlands Information Service, 1968.

Parrillo, Vincent N. "Asian Americans in Asian Politics," in Joseph S. Roucek and Bernard Eisenberg (eds.), *America's Ethnic Politics*. Westport, CT: Greenwood Press, 1982.

———. *Strangers to These Shores*, 3d ed. New York: Macmillan, 1990.

Schulman, Paul. "Can Lady Liberty Ever Say No?" *Sunday Record*, October 6, 1974, p. B1.

Stevens, William K. "Neighbors Rebuff Philadelphia Koreans," *The New York Times*, August 3, 1986, p. 42.

Task Force on the Acculturation of Immigrants to American Life. *The Newest Americans*. New York: American Jewish Committee, 1987.

United Press International (release). "Racial Violence Against Asians Growing in U.S.," November 8, 1987.

U.S. Bureau of the Census. *Current Population Reports*, Series P–25, No. 952. Washington, DC: U.S. Government Printing Office, 1986.

———. *Current Population Reports*, Series P-25, no. 990. Washington, DC: U.S. Government Printing Office, 1987.

———. *Statistical Abstract of the United States: 1987*. Washington, DC: U.S. Government Printing Office, 1988.

U.S. Immigration and Naturalization Service (INS). *Statistical Yearbook: 1989*. Washington, DC: U.S. Government Printing Office, 1990.

Wong, Jan. "Asia Bashing: Bias Against Orientals Increases with Rivalry of Nations' Economies," *The Wall Street Journal*, November 28, 1986, p. 1.

PART TWO

PERCEPTIONS AND REALITIES

3

THE TWILIGHT OF ETHNICITY AMONG AMERICANS OF EUROPEAN ANCESTRY: THE CASE OF THE ITALIANS

Richard D. Alba

The course of ethnicity in advanced industrial societies continues to be debated without satisfactory resolution. Earlier social theorists, inspired by a vision of the erosion of traditional structures under the impact of a tide of modernization, tended to see ethnicity as receding. More recently, sociologists and others have proclaimed the resilience of ethnicity; for some, this is because ethnicity is an affiliation apart, primordial and only superficially modified by currents of modernization, while for others, it is due to ethnicity's moorings in durable structures of inequality.

Proponents of the view that ethnicity is resilient are the dominant voice in contemporary discussions, but their dominance is by no means assured, since the conceptual groundwork for interpreting ethnicity remains unsettled. There is in fact no consensus on the proper vantage point from which to view ethnicity, "assimilation" having been dethroned as the crowning concept of the field in the 1970s and 1980s (Blauner, 1972; Greeley, 1977).

This chapter is reprinted with permission from *Ethnic and Racial Studies*, Vol. 8, No. 1, January 1985, Routledge & Kegan Paul. A preliminary version of this chapter was presented at the 1983 meetings of the American Sociological Association. I am grateful to Robert K. Merton for his comments and to Prentice-Hall for permission to use materials from my book, *Italian Americans: Into the Twilight of Ethnicity*, Englewood Cliffs, NJ: Prentice-Hall, 1985.

This chapter examines some of the interpretive difficulties surrounding ethnicity through the experiences of one group, Italian Americans. In particular, Italians are taken to constitute a strategic test case for some reigning assumptions in the study of ethnicity of European-ancestry groups in the United States. I will argue that the Italian experience demonstrates the importance of boundary-shifting processes, as opposed to assimilation at the invocation of historical contingencies, rooted in structural changes external to the group.

ASSIMILATION AND ETHNIC BOUNDARIES

For a long time, assimilation appeared as one of the most successful and important concepts for the study of ethnicity; this status is reflected in its classic treatment at the hands of Milton Gordon (1964). But much recent writing on ethnicity rejects or avoids assimilation as a focus of major concern. At least part of the reason appears to lie in an implicit model of assimilation, which is ahistorical, individualistic, and incrementalist—which, in other words, does not connect assimilatory processes to macrostructural dynamics but instead conceives of them as individual decisions played out against a static background. Such a conception naturally places the emphasis on social psychological constructs, including the acceptability of a group's members to the majority or core and, perhaps more importantly, their motivation to merge with the majority. At the same time, it is implicitly one-directional: assimilating individuals are affiliating with a new group, thereby dropping the cultural and other garb of their original one.

This individualistic conception makes it easier to understand why assimilation has slipped out of the inner circle of concern. Since it assumes that assimilation hinges on the willingness of individuals to surrender to the majority, then the importance of assimilation would appear to decrease as this willingness does. And this is precisely what seemed to happen during the 1960s in what appeared to many a revival of ethnicity among American groups, both racial minorities and, somewhat surprisingly, those of European ancestry. The revival meant, to use a characterization that, with minor variations, rings throughout the literature on ethnicity in America, that the ethnics were refusing to assimilate (see, for example, Novak, 1972).

One difficulty with this diminishing of the importance of assimilation as a concept is that statistical indicators, such as intermarriage rates (Alba and Chamlin, 1983), suggest the cresting of assimilatory processes in the 1970s and 1980s. The apparent contradiction with the presumed ethnic revival indicates the limitations inherent in the individualistic conception of assimilation and the need to reconceptualize it in a way that allows it to be linked to structural processes of group formation and dissolution. One way to achieve this is explicitly to include the notion of group boundaries within the focus of assimilation. Group boundaries in this context refer to the recognition of ethnic distinctions in interaction and thus are premised upon "criteria for determining membership and ways of signalling membership and exclusion" (Barth, 1969: 15). Ethnic distinctions are socially maintained by such boundary markers as language, speech mannerisms, food, culture (more broadly), and physical appearance, all of which can serve to identify group members to each other and to outsiders.

Reexamining the concept of assimilation with the notion of group boundaries in mind forces the recognition of two ideal types of assimilation. One is the type envisioned by the individualistic conception described above: namely, an individual moves across an ethnic boundary, transferring allegiance to another group, but without any change to the boundary itself. Assimilation of this kind can be viewed as a sort of population trade between different ethnic blocs (see, for example, Newman, 1973; Greeley, 1971). Research advancing such an interpretation has emphasized such consequences of intermarriage as the conversion of one spouse to the religion of the other (Newman, 1973: 162–164). The consequences of this kind of assimilation for ethnic change are problematic; it can be plausibly argued that it does not weaken ethnicity.

The second kind of assimilation is a group form: it is assimilation accomplished through a change in ethnic boundaries, either through a weakening to reduce their salience or through a shift that removes a previously recognized distinction. By definition, such boundary changes mean changes to ethnicity as well. That they may occur is made plausible by the much-noted observation that the coincidence of ethnic and other boundaries, such as those of occupation and residence, tends to enhance ethnic solidarity (Glazer and Moynihan, 1970; Hechter, 1978; Yancey et al., 1976); consequently, a dilution through mobility of ethnic considerations in particular occupational strata or neighborhoods might be expected to weaken ethnic boundaries.

Empirically, of course, there is not necessarily a sharp distinction between the two types. Nonetheless, a separate recognition for the second type is valuable because it forces attention to structural factors that may enhance or detract from ethnic solidarity, such as those stemming from the cultural division of labor (Hechter, 1978), group size (Blau, 1977), and the institutional completeness of ethnic communities (Breton, 1964).

The type of assimilation at the group level also underlines the cardinal importance of studying interethnic relations since they provide a means of detecting ethnic boundaries and the changes that occur to them. The same does not hold true for the "content" of boundaries, that is, the cultural and other signs of group membership, which may change without change to the boundaries themselves (Barth, 1969); for this reason, the study of culture by itself is not decisive for resolving questions of ethnicity. The occurrence, even the frequent occurrence, of interethnic relations also need not contradict the existence of an ethnic boundary, but the maintenance of such a boundary requires that interethnic contacts be asymmetric in some fundamental way, as would be true of relations between members of groups of unequal status (Barth, 1969). Interactions structured by ethnicity help to maintain ethnic distinctions. This is generally not the case for symmetric, nonsegmental relations, such as those of friendship and marriage. A change in the pattern of such relations is a signal of a change in ethnic boundaries.[1]

A CASE IN POINT: ITALIAN AMERICANS

Italian Americans provide an intriguing example of the significance of boundary-shift processes as well as a litmus test for the most frequently advanced interpretations of ethnicity. Thus, those who argue for the persistence or revival of ethnicity generally point to white ethnic groups such as the Italians to support their argument. In this view, Italians remain entrenched in ethnicity partly because of their recency of arrival and partly because their core values—in particular, the values embodied in the family—have enabled them to maintain solid ethnic communities, manifest for example in vital urban neighborhoods.

These contemporary arguments find an echo in older ones. Few argued on behalf of the assimilability of the Italians at the time of their arrival, for they entered as one of the most despised of European immigrant groups (Higham, 1970). The bulk of the Italian immigration before the close of mass immigration in the 1920s came from the rural villages of the south, or Mezzogiorno, although because of the imprecision of both American and Italian statistics, it is not possible to estimate precisely the proportion from southern provinces (Sori, 1979).[2] The available statistics, however, do clearly support the well-known overall picture of an immigration swollen with a dislocated peasantry. For example, tabulations published by the Immigration Commission of 1911 reveal that in the crucial period 1899–1910, when 2.22 million Italian immigrants arrived on American shores (44 percent of the total from 1820 to 1970), 32 percent of those with European work experience described themselves as farm laborers and an additional 43 percent as laborers (Kessner, 1977: 33–34). The general category of "laborer," or *bracciante*, included many who had only recently been forced out of agricultural work (Sori, 1979).

The experiences of southern Italians hardly constituted preparation for integration into an urban, industrial society. The Mezzogiorno presents a classical picture of an underdeveloped society where the penetration of capitalist markets of land and labor created severe dislocations, uprooting peasants from the land, and transforming them into a rural proletariat. By the latter part of the nineteenth century, many rural dwellers were forced to work the land of others, frequently under share-cropping or other tenancy arrangements that gave them little return for their efforts. Patterns of land holding and land use, combined with unfavorable climate and topography, produced an agriculture of scarcity, characterized by chronic shortages of work and food (Covello, 1972; Schneider and Schneider, 1976; Sori, 1979). And the nature of the work bore little relation either to farm or industrial work in the United States. The tools were primitive so that, according to the immigrant writer Constantine Panunzio, "When they come to America, the work which comes nearest to that which they did in Italy is not farming or even farm labor, but excavation work" (Panunzio, 1928: 78; quoted by Kessner, 1977: 39).

The cultural values engendered by the social and material contours of the Mezzogiorno also did not mesh well with the exigencies in the United States. In such a landscape of scarcity, a supreme value was placed on the family. It has been observed many times that the family, not the individual, was the basic social atom of Mezzogiorno society; in the well-known words of Robert Foerster, "Life in the South exalts the family. It has been said of Sicily that the family sentiment is perhaps the only deeply rooted moral sentiment that prevails" (Foerster, 1924: 95). This was not, however, the "amoral familism" of Robert Banfield (1958), who portrays Mezzogiorno life as a Hobbesian war pitting each nuclear family against all others. Southern Italian social structure was constituted in good part from filaments of family-like relations extending beyond the nuclear family, such as extended kinship, fictive kinship created through the institution of godparentship (*compareggio*), and friendship (*amicizia*) (Chapman, 1971; Schneider and Schneider, 1976).

An aspect of the southern Italian ethos with repercussions for Italians in America lay in the presumption that family interests should take precedence over individual ones. A well-known instance of this occurred in relation to marriage. Since the position of a family was affected by the marriages of its members, families attempted to exert considerable control over the choice of a spouse, to the point that many marriages were arranged. Family control was enhanced by the sexual provisions of the Mezzogiorno's code of honor, which drastically restricted contact between eligible men and women (Chapman, 1971). A second instance lay in the economic value attached to children. In peasant families, children were generally expected to make an economic contribution as soon as they were able to work, beginning usually during adolescence. The early initiation to work brought an abrupt transition to adulthood. It also generally spelled the end of formal schooling. This was in any event in accordance with the family-centered culture, in which education was regarded with suspicion, as a potential danger to family solidarity (Covello, 1972: 257; Gambino, 1974).

This occupational and cultural background powerfully shaped the niche the immigrants were able to establish for themselves. The majority of Italian immigrants sought work in urban labor markets, in part because they frequently intended to repatriate after earning enough money to improve their position, and this limited them to places where employment was readily available. But immigrants fresh from the peasantry discovered upon their arrival that only "peek and shuvil" work, as Panunzio described it (quoted by Kessner, 1977: 58), was open to them. In 1905 in New York City, that is, at the height of immigration in the city with the largest concentration of Italians in the United States, nearly 60 percent of Italian household heads did unskilled or semiskilled manual labor, working on construction gangs or as rag pickers and longshoremen (Kessner, 1977: 52–59). The reasons were not limited to a shortage of skills that could be applied in the industrial sector. Culturally engendered expectations about the nature of work, carried from the Mezzogiorno, also constrained occupational possibilities. That many immigrant men took jobs in construction or on the docks was partly a result of a preference for outdoor work, an attempt to reproduce familiar work cycles and conditions. This preference tended to consign Italians to seasonal work outside the regular channels of blue-collar mobility, which were found in factories (Yans-McLaughlin, 1977: 35–44).

Culture also limited the work horizons of women. One of Mezzogiorno's strongest prohibitions was directed against contact between women and male strangers, and this powerful norm went far toward defining what was an acceptable work situation for women. Work in the home was strongly preferred. Some took in boarders (generally relatives or *paesani* in order not to compromise the family honor) and others homework such as laundering or the manufacture of artificial flowers. One instance where Italian women did work outside the home occurred in the New York City garment industry, where women could work among other women (Yans-McLaughlin, 1977: 50–54).

Immigrant adjustment was complicated by the intention to repatriate. The number who ultimately returned to the Mezzogiorno is uncertain, but clearly it was large; one estimate is that 1.5 million Italians returned from the United States in the years between 1900 and 1914 (Caroli, 1973: 41). The sojourner's orientation toward the homeland, felt undoubtedly also by many who stayed, delayed such important adaptations as the acquisition of citizenship and the learning of English.[3] Stanley Lieberson's study of ten cities, for example, shows that in 1930, at a point when new immigration had all but ceased, Italians had the highest percentage of foreign-born who did not speak English in nine of the cities (they ranked second highest in the other); and they had the first or second highest percentages of immigrants who were not citizens in eight cities (Lieberson, 1963: 206–218). Obviously, this retarded adaptation had a large impact on the group, disadvantaging it relative to other immigrant groups who arrived around the same time, particularly in relation to Jews, who did not wish to return to the European societies from which they fled (Kessner, 1977: 167).

The prospects for Italians seemed bleak also on the basis of American reactions to them. The Italian group arrived in a period when racial ideologies were widespread in the United States; and its arrival served to stimulate their further development, as Italians became a focus for explicitly racist thinking and stereotypes. The Italians were perceived as prone to crime, both organized and that spurred by passion and vengeance, the latter symbolized for Americans by the stiletto (Higham, 1970: 66–67). The Italian distinctiveness was perceived in physical terms as well: the immigrants were "swarthy" and seemed to bear other signs of physical degradation, such as low foreheads. In the racially conscious climate, at a time when race theoreticians were attempting to draw biological distinctions among European peoples to the disfavor of those from the south and east, the question of color may have been unavoidable. It would go much too far to say that Italians were viewed as nonwhites, but their color position was problematic. This is evident in the common epithet for them, "guinea," which was derived from a term referring originally to slaves from the western coast of Africa (Mencken, 1963: 373; Craigie and Hulbert, 1940: 1192–1193).

THE SITUATION IN THE 1930s

The assimilability of the Italians continued to seem unlikely in the 1930s, after the close of the period of mass immigration. This is not to deny that significant cultural changes had taken place by then; these were especially evident in the transition to the second generation. Important aspects of the family-centered culture of the Mezzogiorno were so attuned to southern Italian situations that they could not be reestablished successfully in the United States. For example, strict control over unmarried daughters was only workable in southern Italian villages, where parents were in a position to evaluate the suitability of all potential suitors. Parental superiority broke down in American ghettos since more acculturated children were better able to make appropriate matches for themselves. The extent of change in family norms is suggested by Caroline Ware's study of Greenwich Village in the early 1930s (Ware, 1935: 180–202). In a survey of its Italian residents, she found clear-cut differences between older and younger respondents, a division that no doubt corresponded well with generational status (that is, foreign versus native-born). Older Italians were less likely than younger ones to reject such Mezzogiorno family norms as "girls should not associate with men unless engaged" and parental arrangement of marriages.

But in other ways, the same survey indicates second-generation fidelity to the southern Italian cultural heritage. Only half of the younger group rejected the proposition that "a child should sacrifice his personal ambition to the welfare of the family group," and only 15 percent denied that "children owe absolute obedience to parents" (Ware, 1935: 193).

One area in which the remaining power of the family ethos was undeniably manifest was that of education. The conflict between the school system and the family that had existed in the Mezzogiorno was renewed in America. Immigrant families perceived many points of friction in the contact between these culturally alien worlds. These occurred even in seemingly innocuous matters such as school recreation, which immigrant parents saw as creating moral and physical risks for teenagers, who in their eyes were already adults (Covello, 1972: 325–326).

Undoubtedly, the most important conflict centered on the economic contribution expected of children, which was jeopardized
by compulsory attendance laws, greatly resented by Italian parents.

As a result of the clash between school and family, Italian
children had high rates of truancy and frequently left school as
early as the law allowed (Covello, 1972). In fact, during the
height of mass immigration, it is estimated that as many as 10
percent of the immigrant children in New York City managed
to avoid school altogether (Kessner, 1977: 96). But even as late
as 1930, only 11 percent of Italian Americans who entered New
York City high schools graduated from them, at a time when
over 40 percent of all the city's high school students stayed
through to receive their diplomas (Covello, 1972: 285). The obvious consequence was low ultimate educational attainment for
second-generation Italians and a channeling of them toward jobs
where educational credentials were not important, mostly in the
blue-collar ranks.

The ultimate assimilation of the Italians was also put in question by attitudes of the Italians themselves. Two studies of Italian-American ghettos, in Boston and New Haven, offer relevant
testimony. William Foote Whyte's (1955) classic study indicates
a split among Italians in their attitudes toward assimilation. He
portrays the division in terms of "college boys," oriented toward
mobility into the larger society, and "corner boys," loyal to their
peer groups and held on ghetto corners by that loyalty. Whyte
did not provide direct evidence on the relative popularity of
these two orientations, but Irvin Child's (1943) New Haven study
did. Child depicted the attitudes of Italians as defined against a
background of virulent prejudice directed at their group, which
hedged in the possible choices with the risk of potential losses.
Identification with the Italian group meant risking complete exclusion by other Americans and the loss of any prospects for
mobility. On the other hand, identification with Americans, and
hence a positive valuation of assimilation, risked a double rejection: by non-Italians as a result of prejudice and by other
Italians on the grounds of disloyalty to the group. According to
Child, the most common response to this double-bind situation
was one he labeled "apathetic": a denial of the meaningfulness

of nationality distinctions and of the existence of prejudice against Italians. Individuals displaying the apathetic response remained through inertia within the orbit of Italian-American social and cultural life, for it required deliberate action to break this social gravity and move into non-Italian spheres. Because of the risks involved, few maintained such intentions.

THE 1940s AND 50s: THE WATERSHED

By the end of the 1930s, an analysis based solely on the group's experiences and its cultural and occupational background would seem to have doomed Italian Americans to a perpetual position of inferiority and separateness in American society. But such an analysis would have been misleading because other developments were taking place in the larger society that affected the context within which Italian-American preferences would be played out. These factors came to a head during and shortly after World War II.

Some had been in the background all along, but the war sharpened their effects. One such factor was the transformation of the occupational structure and the attendant structural mobility. Between 1930 and 1970, for example, the white-collar proportion of the national labor force expanded rapidly from 29.4 percent to 44.8 percent (all figures are from U.S. Bureau of the Census, 1975: 139); about half this change, moreover, was concentrated in the upper part of the white-collar spectrum, the category of professional and technical workers, whose share of the labor force increased in this period from 6.8 percent to 13.7 percent. Although the proportion in the combined blue-collar and service occupations hardly changed, within them a significant realignment was taking shape. In particular, unskilled laborers, a category that included many Italian Americans in the earlier part of the century, declined sharply from 11.0 percent to 4.4 percent. The structural mobility engendered by such shifts in the occupational distribution holds a special significance for disadvantaged ethnic groups because it does not have a "zero sum" character. Thus, the upward mobility of an individual or group can occur without the complementary downward mobility of another; and as a result, it is not likely to produce a heightened salience of group boundaries among more advantaged groups, intended to keep the disadvantaged in their place.

The effects wrought by structural mobility were most sharply felt in those places where Italian Americans were concentrated: the metropolitan areas of the north. This is made clearest by examining the kinds of jobs that were opening up and closing out in different places in the postwar interval since it is the changes at the margins that chiefly dictate the occupational options for young people entering the labor force and thus shape intergenerational occupational mobility. Over the period 1940–1960, metropolitan areas in general were the places of greatest job growth (Stanback and Knight, 1970). In the older metropolises of the northeast and midwest, growth was primarily concentrated in white-collar rather than blue-collar jobs (Barry and Kasarda, 1977: chapter 12).

A corollary of structural occupational shifts during the 1940s and 1950s was another kind of structural mobility: the rapid expansion of higher education and its transformation from a selective system to a mass one. In 1940, only 15 percent of the college-age group actually attended college, but by 1954 the rate of college attendance had climbed to 30 percent; by 1960, it was almost 38 percent (Trow, 1961). This expansion played an important role in reducing status differences because, in addition to propelling occupational mobility, higher education extends a sense of equality among its students through an experience that is viewed as a sharp alteration in status and is sanctified by the selectivity of colleges and universities.

World War II acted as a catalyst for both kinds of mobility. The war helped to drag the United States out of the Depression and opened up an era of prosperity and economic growth, signaled by a steady growth in real income beginning in the early 1950s (Miller, 1971); and it specifically fueled the expansion of higher education through the G.I. Bill. But the impact of the war had a powerful effect on American perceptions of nationality and national origins.

The crux of the wartime situations during this century is that they have turned ethnic identity into a matter of national loyalty, thereby giving ethnicity a subversive appearance and ultimately hastening a deemphasis on nationality differences. The diversity of the origins of Americans and the substantial proportion of those of recent origins, particularly from combatant nations, have made Americans sensitive to the potential frailty of national solidarity. During World War I, the presence of millions of recently arrived European immigrants provoked intense anxieties about the immediate loyalties of aliens and the potential for subversion from within, leading to overt xenophobia and demands for the "pressure-cooker assimilation" and "100 percent Americanization" of the immigrants (Higham, 1970). By the 1940s, the flood tide of immigration had receded; the groups with the potential for loyalty to enemy nations were increasingly composed of the native-born, and the responses of Americans were accordingly different.

This is not to say that the war did not stimulate anxieties over national loyalty. The internment of Japanese Americans demonstrates indisputably that it did. In the case of European ethnics, clouds of suspicion gathered early during the war over Germans and Italians but then largely gave way to a cultivated national unity that was also a response to the wartime strains. The melding of Americans of different nationalities was almost ritualistically promoted by festivals to celebrate the contributions of immigrant groups to America (Polenberg, 1980: 54). More significant, wartime reporting and films about the war made for domestic consumption self-consciously highlighted the spirit of unity among American fighting men from different backgrounds, portraying the armed forces as a melting pot in miniature (Blum, 1976: 63).

The war no doubt served to drive home the perils of too strong an ethnic identification for many ethnics. One of Child's New Haven respondents sharply formulated a general problem: "Then a lot of times in the show you see Mussolini on the screen and they all start to razz him. Then I feel, 'How the hell do I stand?' " (Child, 1943: 88).

A frequent response on the part of the ethnics was a push toward further assimilation. Ethnics had high rates of enlistment in the military, and there was massive adoption of American citizenship by the foreign-born—more than 1.75 million became citizens in the period 1940–1945 (Polenberg, 1980: 57). Movement toward acculturation is evident in the waning of the foreign language press that occurred during the war. The number of radio stations broadcasting in immigrant languages dropped by 40 percent between 1942 and 1948 (Polenberg, 1980: 55).

An ultimate impact of the war was to render the perceptions of the ethnics more fluid and thus open to the possibility of change. One realm in which this influence is visible is in the novels about the war, published during it and afterwards. Norman Mailer's *The Naked and the Dead*, James Jones's *From Here to Eternity*, Harry Brown's *A Walk in the Sun*, and John Hersey's *A Bell for Adano*, which were all popular novels made into successful films, presented a very different version of American society from that which prevailed before the war. Like many wartime films, these novels depicted military groups that contained American ethnic diversity, or more precisely the part of European ancestry in microcosm, and showed ethnics as the moral equals of those of "old stock" origins (Blum, 1976). The novels, which served to interpret the war experience for many Americans, signaled a shift in attitudes toward ethnics.

Thus, World War II stands as a watershed for European ethnics, partly because it lies at a fortuitous conjunction of forces—structural transformation of the labor force, demographic transition from the immigrant to the second generation among the ethnics of recent European origins, and a cultural relaxation of the attitudes toward ethnics—that served to fluidify the boundaries separating ethnics from "old stock" groups. It remains still to confirm that these massive forces actually had an effect on the life chances of ethnics. Relevant evidence is supplied by Lieberson's more recent study, which reveals a prodigious socioeconomic leap for the 1925–1935 cohort of second-generation south-central and eastern European ethnics, which came to maturity during and shortly after the war (Lieberson, 1980: 200–206, 328–332).

The boundary fluidity associated with the large-scale mobility in the aftermath of the war was further advanced by the enormous residential movements of the 1950s and 1960s. In the single decade from 1950 to 1960, the population in the suburbs increased by nearly 50 percent, from 41 million to 60 million (Polenberg, 1980: 128). For ethnics and others, the suburban exodus was often directly connected with occupational chances—and not merely the result of increasing affluence—since the bulk of newly created jobs were to be found in the suburban fringes, not in central-city areas (Berry and Kasarda, 1977: chapter 12). But the exodus was full of portent for ethnic groups because it disrupted urban ethnic communities and brought many mobile families into an ethnically heterogeneous milieu, a shift with obvious ramifications for the next generation. The residential changes of Italians are exemplified by the group's distribution in the metropolitan region centered around New York City and Newark, New Jersey, which contained nearly a third of the Italian Americans counted in the 1970 Census. By then, the second generation had significantly dispersed to the suburbs. According to Census figures, 47 percent were living in the area's smaller towns, those with fewer than 100,000 residents; and 41 percent were living in places with fewer than 50,000. These figures are only slightly lower than those for whites generally (50 percent and 45 percent, respectively). However, first-generation Italians remained distinctly more concentrated in the region's larger cities. Only 35 percent were in places smaller than 100,000 in population and 29 percent in places smaller than 50,000.[4]

Obviously, the changes of the postwar period did not mean a complete dissolution of ethnic communities and subcultures. Herbert Gans's (1962) study of Boston's West End in the late 1950s establishes that many, particularly in the urban working class, remained firmly in the grip of ethnic worlds. But a process had been initiated, one that spelled a gradual lowering of ethnic boundaries among European ancestry groups and an upward shift in the life chances of their younger members.

THE CONTEMPORARY SITUATION OF ITALIAN AMERICANS

This process of boundary shifts has had a profound impact on Italian Americans, and recent evidence points to a convergence with other European ancestry groups, including those of older stock. As one demonstration, consider the educational trajectory across different cohorts of second- and later-generation Italians, compiled in Table 3.1 from the November 1979

Table 3.1

Rates of College Education among Italian Americans, by Sex, Generation, and Cohort and Compared to Those of Third-Generation British Americans

Men

Cohort	Second generation % attended college	Second generation % finished 4 or more yrs.	Third generation % attended college	Third generation % finished 4 or more yrs.	Third-generation British Americans % attended college	Third-generation British Americans % finished 4 or more yrs.
1951-	56.6	28.9	54.4	25.8	53.2	27.1
1946-50	42.1	32.8	55.9	29.1	66.4	38.1
1941-45	45.4	26.2	51.8	35.7	55.7	38.5
1936-40	42.9	30.3	42.3	22.1	51.5	35.1
1931-35	33.0	18.7	39.0	18.4	50.3	31.3
1926-30	24.9	11.7	31.5	15.2	42.1	27.8
1921-25	22.1	16.0	20.1	7.7	43.9	23.8
1916-20	17.5	3.9	13.4	11.3	35.7	20.1
-15	16.3	7.9	15.2	6.2	30.1	17.4

Women

Cohort	Second generation % attended college	Second generation % finished 4 or more yrs.	Third generation % attended college	Third generation % finished 4 or more yrs.	Third-generation British Americans % attended college	Third-generation British Americans % finished 4 or more yrs.
1951-	50.4	20.2	46.6	26.3	48.8	24.0
1946-50	35.0	17.1	40.5	20.0	53.5	31.8
1941-45	27.3	13.1	32.1	13.5	44.7	22.5
1936-40	28.3	13.2	18.2	3.9	39.0	21.7
1931-35	9.1	4.4	17.9	10.5	33.2	16.1
1926-30	14.6	5.7	27.6	9.2	41.8	23.0
1921-25	8.2	4.5	22.6	5.1	29.7	14.5
1916-20	7.0	4.2	30.1	20.2	37.6	17.8
-15	5.1	1.8	2.7	0.0	26.5	12.3

Source: Calculated from U.S. Bureau of the Census, 1982.

Table restricted to individuals older than 22. The "third generation" contains all native-born group members with native-born parents and thus encompasses the third and later generations.

Current Population Survey.[5] To provide a rigorous yardstick against which to measure change, comparable figures are also provided for third- and later-generation Americans of exclusively British ancestry (defined as those who report ancestry only from England, Scotland, and Wales). Such a comparison group avoids the confusion that might be introduced by including other recent ethnics in the reference group and also compares the Italians to an ethnic category that is indisputably part of the American core, thus underlining the sharpness of the changes. For similar reasons, the focus in the table is exclusively on rates of college attendance and graduation.

What stands out in the table is a pattern of convergence across cohorts. Although the pattern is complicated somewhat by an unsustained peak in college education among British Americans in the 1946–1950 cohort (which may be part of a Vietnam-era phenomenon revealed by a recent Census report) and by some wandering of the numbers from a simple trajectory of linear change, its basic nature is clear: a gradual narrowing of Italian differences from British Americans and the achievement of parity in the youngest cohort (who were in their midtwenties in 1979). This convergence holds for both men and women, and indeed what the table also reveals is the relatively greater disadvantage of Italian-American women in the past, especially in the second generation. For this last group, the rise in college attendance (from 9.1 percent to 50.4 percent) across a twenty-year time span, from the 1931–1935 cohort to that of 1951–1956, is very strong. The convergence also holds for both generations, and underlining the historical nature of the convergence is the fact that the generations do not seem much different, although the third generation shows some tendency to take the lead in rising rates of college attendance.

Evidence of cultural convergence is provided by survey items that tap attitudes and values connected with the stereotypical family-centered ethos presumed to color Italian-American life (see, for example, Greeley and McCready, 1975).[6] One widely cited expression of this is greater loyalty to kin groups, purportedly evident for instance in a reluctance to move away from the family (Gambino, 1974; Vecoli, 1978). Another is conservatism on family-related matters, ranging from hostility toward

Table 3.2
Cultural Comparison between WASPs and Italian Americans

	WASP mean	Italian mean	difference	diff. after adjustment[a]
Anti-abortion scale	1.33	1.42	.09	.20*
Anti-feminism scale	1.26	1.25	−.01	.08
Premarital sex is 'always wrong'	34.5%	22.6%	−11.9*	1.3
Adultery is 'always wrong'	69.8%	58.6%	−11.2*	−3.5
Homosexual sex is 'always wrong'	69.3%	60.4%	−8.9*	−4.7
Ever divorced or legally separated	25.7%	21.9%	−3.8	−4.4
Divorce should be 'more difficult'	50.1%	41.3%	−8.8*	−3.1
Scale of value put on self-direction for children	1.24	1.17	−.07	−.12
Young people 'should be taught by their elders'	37.9%	53.0%	15.1*	19.8*
Reside in same place where grew up	39.5%	53.2%	13.6*	6.6*
Socialize with relatives weekly	33.8%	46.8%	13.0*	10.4*

Source: Tabulations from the National Opinion Research Center (NORC) General
     Social Surveys, 1975–1980.

*Indicates statistical significance.

[a]Variables for which adjustment has been made include: current region and size
     of place and those where respondent grew up, education and occupation
     of respondent and parents, age, and sex.

changes in sexual mores and the position of women to a low
frequence of divorce (Greeley, 1974; Femminella and Quadagno,
1976).

The thinness of any residual cultural patina among individuals
of Italian heritage is evident from Table 3.2, which reports the
analysis of items from the General Social Surveys for the years
1975 through 1980 (the table is a selection from a larger set
discussed in Alba, 1985).[7] The comparison is again to those of
British ancestry (more precisely, since the General Social Surveys
ask for the religion in which a respondent was raised, the comparison group contains those with Protestant ancestry from the
British Isles). The table presents the comparison without any
controls and also with controls for current region and size of
place as well as those where the respondent was raised, education and occupation of respondent and parents, sex, and age.[8]

On items relating to traditional family roles, Italians are generally quite similar to WASPs. They do not significantly differ

from WASPs in terms of acceptance of abortion, for example, although they appear slightly more conservative after controls are applied because of their greater concentration in areas where liberal attitudes prevail.[9] Italians do not differ from WASPs in their acceptance of women outside the home.[10] Similarity between the groups is also found, albeit with an important exception, in attitudes toward the raising of children. Italians have been depicted as emphasizing traditional values rather than those of self-direction (Rosen, 1959; Schooler, 1976). But in terms of their rating of the desirability of various traits in children, they are not meaningfully different from British Protestants.[11] Worthy of mention for its echo of the Mezzogiorno is one trait on the list, "that he [the child] obeys his parents well." Just a quarter of the Italian-American respondents prize obedience as one of the most desirable traits in children, a figure not statistically different from that for WASPs (28 percent). The exception to this general similarity concerns whether young people should be taught "by their elders to do what is right" or "to think for themselves even though they may do something their elders disapprove of." About half of Italians agree with the position consistent with the family-centered ethos—namely, that young people should be taught by their elders—compared to 38 percent of WASPs. Nonetheless, the Italian percentage is not far from the one for all Americans, 45 percent of whom favor the traditional option.

Despite their conservative image, Italians are more liberal than WASPs in certain respects, apparently because of their location in the metropolitan northeast, where cosmopolitan outlooks are frequent. They are less likely to condemn adultery, premarital sex, and homosexuality as "always wrong." They are also less likely to feel that divorce laws should be tightened to make divorce more difficult to obtain. (The proportion who have ever been divorced or separated is also, incidentally, not statistically different from that found among British Americans.) But in all these cases, the differences disappear after statistical controls are introduced, and an inspection of the regressions indicates that the reduction is chiefly brought about by the controls for place.

Broadly speaking, then, there is little support for the image of a distinctive Italian conservatism on family matters. Where there does appear to be greater evidence for an Italian-American ethos is in terms of loyalty to the family group, but at best its remaining strength seems no more than moderate. This loyalty can be examined through two items in Table 3.2.

One tests the idea that Italians remain rooted in one place because of their reluctance to move away from family. Indeed, an impressive 53 percent reside in the same place where they grew up; however, the percentage of WASPs who do so also is high, 40 percent. Moreover, the Italian percentage could be expected to be higher on the grounds that Italians have more frequently grown up in the cosmopolitan magnets that attract others from their hometowns (New York City is the prototype) and also have lower overall educational and occupational attainment, factors associated with less residential mobility. When controls are applied, the difference between the two groups is only modest, seven percentage points.[12]

Finally, the Italian pattern of socializing with relatives, emphasized by Gans (1962) in his depiction of the "peer group society," still persists to some degree. Nearly half of Italians socialize with family members weekly or more frequently, compared to only a third of WASPs. This difference is not explained very much by the background variables, as the tendency to socialize within the family is not much affected by socioeconomic variables, and this is counterbalanced for WASPs by the fact that it is somewhat higher among those who live in smaller places. After controls, Italians are still 10 percent more likely to socialize on a weekly basis with relatives.

Thus, what remains of the family-centered ethos is a slightly greater tendency to remain in the same place, greatly diluted from ancestral peasant rootedness, and a moderately greater willingness to keep company with relatives. The evidence of cultural convergence seems substantial,[13] but there is still more imposing evidence of convergence and assimilation, as evidenced in intermarriage rates. Intermarriage stands as the cardinal indicator of boundary shift for several reasons (see Merton, 1941). To begin with the obvious, because marriage is an enduring and intimate relation, intermarriage provides a stringent test of group perceptions and of the social distance between

Italians and others. Moreover, an intermarriage is not simply an isolated crossing of ethnic boundaries but carries far wider ramification, including most importantly those for the next generation, which will be raised in an ethnically heterogeneous milieu. Finally, the occurrence of intermarriage implies the occurrence of other relations that penetrate ethnic boundaries.

The intermarriage rates of Italians, calculated from the 1979 Current Population Survey, are presented in Table 3.3. In the case of marriage, it makes little sense to combine individuals of part Italian ancestry with those of wholly Italian parentage, because the social contexts in which the two types are raised are so different that their intermarriage rates are likely to be as well; and consequently, they are shown separately in the table. The marriage rates are also decomposed by generations and birth cohort and are presented separately for men and women.

The table indicates a rapid rise in the intermarriage rate, which has reached the point that, of Italians marrying recently, generally two-thirds to three-quarters, depending on the category of the group, have intermarried. Revealing of the changes is the trend by birth cohort for persons with unmixed Italian ancestry, especially in the second generation. Among those born before 1920, that is, during the era of mass immigration, about 60 percent of this second generation chose spouses of wholly Italian percentage. But this strict endogamy falls off with each new cohort. Among men, a sharp drop occurs with the cohort born during the 1930s; for women, such a drop occurs with the cohort born in the next decade. This rapid change has, among men, closed the gap between the second and third generations. For both, only about 20 percent of men born since 1950 have chosen wives with all Italian parentage, while another 10 to 15 percent have chosen wives with part Italian ancestry. The gap between the generations is not quite closed among women; second-generation women have the highest rate of endogamy in the youngest cohort, although this may be a statistical aberration since a small number of cases is involved. In any event, the great majority of Italian Americans in this cohort belong to the third or later generations, where high intermarriage rates prevail.

Individuals of wholly Italian ancestry provide a conservative estimate of intermarriage rates. Individuals of mixed background

Table 3.3
Marriage Patterns of Italian Americans, by Sex, Generation, and Cohort

	Men			
	Second generation		Third generation	
Cohort	Ancestry of spouse is . . .		Ancestry of spouse is . . .	
	wholly	wholly	wholly	wholly
Ancestry type	Italian %	non-Italian %	Italian %	non-Italian %
1950–				
wholly Ital.	20.3	64.1	20.0	70.5
partly Ital.	–a	–a	5.4	78.9
1940–49				
wholly Ital.	30.0	60.0	24.4	69.2
partly Ital.	0.0	82.7	10.7	76.8
1930–39				
wholly Ital.	29.8	62.9	24.1	63.3
partly Ital.	17.8	81.5	6.9	80.1
1920–29				
wholly Ital.	44.6	51.7	38.8	60.9
partly Ital.	15.7	83.7	4.8	90.0
Before 1920				
wholly Ital.	56.7	41.7	42.7	57.3
partly Ital.	–a	–a	15.8	78.6

	Women			
	Second generation		Third generation	
Cohort	Ancestry of spouse is . . .		Ancestry of spouse is . . .	
	wholly	wholly	wholly	wholly
Ancestry type	Italian %	non-Italian %	Italian %	non-Italian %
1950–				
wholly Ital.	38.7	53.2	23.8	72.7
partly Ital.	–a	–a	10.3	79.1
1940–49				
wholly Ital.	25.7	71.3	31.7	58.4
partly Ital.	20.7	72.1	11.7	77.8
1930–39				
wholly Ital.	38.8	61.0	49.4	46.6
partly Ital.	17.0	83.0	17.2	75.6
1920–29				
wholly Ital.	54.9	44.6	34.6	61.7
partly Ital.	10.3	89.7	18.6	69.3
Before 1920				
wholly Ital.	59.5	37.6	40.8	60.2
partly Ital.	–a	–a	11.5	78.5

Source: Calculated from U.S. Bureau of the Census, 1982.

aPercent not reported because it is based on ten or fewer cases (weighted).

have higher intermarriage rates and, moreover, the overall Italian rates will increasingly resemble theirs since the group is more and more composed of them. For example, if the two ancestry groups are combined among men, then nearly three-quarters of third-generation men born since 1950 have chosen wives with no Italian ancestry. The comparable third-generation figure among women is nearly identical to that for the men.

It might be argued that these high intermarriage rates do not establish by themselves a relaxing of boundaries between Italians and other groups because they do not show whom Italians marry when they marry outside. Thus, it remains possible that other boundaries, enclosing clusters of culturally and socially similar groups, constrain their choices. It is true that, like other European ancestry groups, Italians are very unlikely to marry Hispanics and nonwhites (Alba and Golden, 1984). But this important exception aside, two pieces of evidence damage the thesis of selective intermarriage. One is Richard Alba and Ronald Kessler's (1979) analysis of marriage patterns among Catholics, demonstrating that very little selectivity is visible among those who marry across nationality lines. The second emerges from data that reveal fairly high rates of marriage across religious lines. For example, Alba (1985) shows from General Social Survey data that about half of Italian Catholics born since World War II have married Protestants. So, in other words, it appears that the elective affinities of intermarrying Italians are not narrowly channeled to a few groups but range widely across the spectrum of European ancestries.

The rising rate of intermarriage is bringing about a profound transformation of the Italian ancestry group. The character of this transformation is quite evident when the proportion of individuals with mixed Italian ancestry is displayed by birth cohort, as is done in Table 3.4.[14] The figures reveal a striking relationship of mixed parentage to cohort, with a percentage change between the oldest and youngest cohorts of over 75 percent. These dramatic figures indicate that a tremendous swing in the nature of the Italian ancestry group is destined to take place by the end of this century, as members of older cohorts, for the most part of unmixed ancestry, die and are replaced by younger persons of mixed parentage. Thus, in the

Table 3.4
Type of Italian Ancestry by Age (1979)

	% with mixed Italian ancestry
all ages	48.0
65 and over	5.9
55 to 64	11.4
45 to 54	18.5
35 to 44	36.1
25 to 34	48.1
18 to 24	60.5
14 to 17	71.3
5 to 13	77.8
under 5	81.5

Source: U.S. Bureau of the Census, 1982: Table 2.

Current Population Survey, persons with only Italian ancestry make up two-thirds of the adult ancestry group, a comfortable majority. But counting individuals of all ages, including children, they were a scant majority: 52 percent. Taking into account the expected mortality in the older group, these figures suggest that individuals with one non-Italian parent will compose a majority of the ancestry group by the end of the 1990s.

It is doubtful that even the mild distinctiveness of Italians on matters of family solidarity can withstand such higher intermarriage rates. Intermarriage not only tests the extent of existing cultural differences among groups, but it ultimately alters the cultural boundary. Colleen Leahy Johnson's (1982) study of kinship contact among Italians in Syracuse, New York, illustrates the general process. She compared in-married and out-married Italians to each other and to Protestants of non-Italian background in terms of the frequency of their contact with parents, siblings, and other relatives. Although contact with the relatives on the Italian side appeared dominant among the intermarried Italians, in the sense that both spouses saw more of them than of the non-Italian relatives, the frequency of contact was diminished; the intermarried group stood intermediate between the in-married Italians, the majority of whom had daily contact with parents and with siblings, and the Protestants, the majority of whom had comparatively infrequent contact with their relatives. Johnson's research implies that high rates of intermarriage are associated with further erosion of what Gans labeled as the "peer group society" in the 1950s.

CONCLUSION

Italian Americans are on the verge of the twilight of their ethnicity. "Twilight" appears an accurate metaphor for a stage when ethnic differences will remain visible, but only faintly so. The metaphor acknowledges the claims of many (see, for example, Glazer and Moynihan, 1970; Greeley, 1977) that indeed ethnicity has not speedily disappeared and, therefore, the optimism of the melting-pot portrayal of American society seems to have been ill-founded. At the same time, it also captures the reality that ethnicity, at least among whites, seems to be steadily receding.

The approach of this twilight may seem deceiving, for when Italians and some other white ethnic groups are observed in the aggregate, their ethnic features still appear prominent. But in the case of the Italians, this happens because earlier generations and older cohorts are quite different from old-stock Americans on such factors as educational and occupational attainment. Hence, it is only when the group is analytically decomposed by generation or birth cohort that the leading edge of change can be discerned.

Properly analyzed, the evidence on behalf of the looming ethnic twilight among Italians appears overwhelming. Despite the widely accepted image of an intense, family-centered Italian-American culture, the group's cultural distinctiveness has paled to a feeble version of its former self. Paralleling this change, the social boundary between Italians and other Americans has become easily permeable; intermarriage, an irrevocable indicator of boundary shifts, takes place quite freely between Italians and those of other European ancestries. Acculturation and social assimilation have been fed by a surge in the educational attainment of Italians, which has brought cohorts born since World War II to the brink of parity with British Americans, the quintessential

American group. Moreover, this profound transformation of the Italian group has taken place at a time when the fourth generation, the first generation without direct contact with the immigrant experience, is small (Steinberg, 1982; Alba, 1985). But this generation will grow substantially in size during the rest of this century, and simultaneously, the first and second generations, which presently constitute the majority of the group, will shrink.

In a number of respects, events among the Italians seem to parallel those among other groups descended from European immigrants, although because of differences in their times of arrival, the specific situation that greeted them, and their occupational and cultural heritages, no two groups are following exactly the same pathways to the twilight stage. Yet among virtually all white ethnic groups, one can observe a progressive, if gradual, dampening of cultural distinctiveness. Core values have been overwhelmed by a common American culture so that even though cultural uniformity has not been the end result, the remaining differences among groups are so mild as to constitute neither a basis for group solidarity nor a barrier to intergroup contact.

Additionally, among almost all groups, one can see a spreading pattern of intermarriage, testimony to the minor nature of remaining group differences and guarantee of additional assimilation (see, for example, Alba, 1976). The strength of this pattern is confirmed by events among Jewish Americans, who provide the acid test of pervasive intermarriage. Historically, the rate of Jewish-Gentile intermarriage rate has been quite low, but recent studies have confirmed a sharp rise in this rate, starting in the 1960s (Cohen, 1983).

Such pervasive intermarriage suggests the emergence of a new ethnic group, one defined by ancestry from anywhere on the European continent. This need not mean that ethnic differences within this group will disappear altogether, but rather that their character is being fundamentally altered. This appears to be increasingly the case with ethnic identity. As Gans (1979) has observed, many mobile ethnics attempt to maintain some psychological connection with their origins but in such a way that this attachment does not prevent them from mixing freely with others of diverse backgrounds. This contemporary form of ethnicity is private and voluntary, intermittent and undemanding; it focuses on symbols of ethnic cultures rather than the cultures themselves and tends to be confined to leisure-time activities. There is a wide latitude available for this "symbolic ethnicity"— for Italians, it can range from a liking for pasta to a repudiation of criminal stereotypes—but the crucial point is that it is the individual who decides on the appropriate form. Such an ethnic identity is, in other words, a personal style and not the manifestation of membership in an ethnic group.

The impending twilight of ethnicity among those of European ancestry is not matched by equal changes among most of America's non-European minorities. Black Americans stand as the extreme case. Though their socioeconomic progress in recent years has been debated, no informed observer claims that they are even close to parity with whites (Farley, 1985). It hardly needs saying, then, that racial boundaries remain silent. Residentially, blacks are still extremely segregated from whites, and the incidence of black-white intermarriage is very small (Heer, 1980).

The position of some other minorities is more ambiguous. Some older non-European groups that were voluntary immigrants to the United States evidence developments like those among the white ethnics, though these are not as far along. For example, Japanese Americans, despite the bitter legacy of World War II internment, have been quite successful in socioeconomic terms, with high rates of college attendance and occupational mobility. In tandem with this upward movement have come increases in intermarriage, frequently with whites (Montero, 1981; Woodrum, 1981). Although in the future it may become appropriate to speak of an ethnic twilight among Japanese Americans, the picture for non-European groups is complicated by the large-scale immigration from Asia, the Caribbean, and Latin America since immigration laws were revised in 1965. Immigrants from Colombia, Cuba, Haiti, Korea, Mexico, the Philippines, Taiwan, Hong Kong, Vietnam, and still other places are adding new parts to the American ethnic tapestry. Thus, although twilight may be descending on those ethnic groups whose forebears came from Europe, ethnicity itself is not subsiding as an issue for American society. In the future, the salient ethnic outlines may stem from non-European origins, just as those of European origins have been prominent in the recent past.

NOTES

1. This, of course, coincides with the importance that Gordon (1964) attributes to "structural assimilation," that is, large-scale primary relations across ethnic boundaries.

2. Although American immigration authorities began to keep statistics on "southern" and "northern" Italians in 1899, the racial intent of the distinction distorted the definition of a "southern" Italian to include anyone from the "peninsula proper" (as well as the islands of Sicily and Sardinia). According to the Bureau of Immigration's definition, "even Genoa is South Italian" (U.S. Senate, 1911: 81). While American statistics were weakened in this way, Italian statistics depended largely on applications for the *nulla osta*, or exit permit, which required a destination to be stated. But many applicants either did not subsequently leave or went somewhere other than where they stated (Caroli, 1973: 30; Sori, 1979). Nonetheless, both sources, though imprecise, are broadly consistent.

3. Jerre Mangione's (1981) memoir of Italian-American life in Rochester paints a very clear portrait of the sojourner's mentality among his Sicilian relatives.

4. These figures are for the New York, Northeastern New Jersey Standard Consolidated Area, which in 1970 contained 1.4 million foreign-stock Italian Americans. The figures are my calculations from Tables 17, 23, and 81 of the *Characteristics of the Population*, Parts 32 and 34 (U.S. Bureau of the Census, 1973).

5. This survey included the same ethnic ancestry question that appeared in the long form of the 1980 Census. This question, "What is ___'s ancestry?" is superior to questions asked in previous Current Population Surveys and decennial Censuses because it does not constrain answers by a predefined list of responses and hence does not eliminate the many individuals with mixed ancestry. However, by the same token, it offers a too inclusive definition of the Italian-American group, since it forces the inclusion of individuals with any reported degree of Italian ancestry, regardless of its magnitude and of the extent of their identification with the Italian group (for a more detailed discussion, see Alba, 1985). A virtue of this survey for the study of socioeconomic change is that its large sample size allows for refined breakdowns.

6. The focus here must be on this ethos rather than the outward forms of culture since these tend to wither away within the first two generations. This is true, for example, of the everyday-use of the Italian language. According to the Current Population Survey, over 4 million claim Italian as a mother tongue, a language spoken in their childhood home, but only 1.4 million (about 12 percent of the group) claim to speak it in their current home (U.S. Bureau of the Census, 1982: 14). Since the total size of the ancestry group is around 12 million and that of the first generation, whose members are very likely to continue to speak their native tongue at home, is 800 thousand, it is clear that only a small part of the second and third generations continues to use the language on an everyday basis. For further analysis of external culture, see James Crispino (1980).

7. The General Social Surveys offer a narrower definition of the Italian-American group than does the November 1979 Current Population Survey. The GSS ask individuals with mixed ethnic ancestry to identify, if they can, the group to which they feel closer. This is then reported as their ethnic category.

8. The adjusted difference between the groups reported in the table is the coefficient for the Italian dummy variable taken from a regression analysis. To achieve stable estimates of the effects of the control variables, the regression analysis includes all whites; the comparison to WASPs is effected by making them the omitted category.

9. The value of the antiabortion scale is the number of times the respondent would deny a legal abortion in three situations where a presumably healthy pregnancy has resulted from voluntary sexual activity (Davis et al., 1980: 143–144). Such situations are the litmus test for abortion attitudes, as most Americans would allow an abortion for such circumstances as a life-endangering pregnancy or one resulting from rape.

10. The antifeminism scale is a summative scale composed of responses to four questions such as, "Do you approve or disapprove of a married woman earning money in business or industry if she has a husband capable of supporting her?" For the wording of the other three, see James Davis et al. (1980: 142).

11. These items are derived from the well-known ones developed by Melvin Kohn and his colleagues. But there is no pretense here of replicating Kohn's work, since he has explicitly confined the validity of his scale to parents with children in a certain age range (Kohn, 1976). Such a limitation is not feasible here.

The scale reported here is calculated by counting a +1 for each time a respondent rated as desirable a trait associated with self-direction and also each time he or she rated as undesirable a trait associated with conformity, and counting a -1 when the reverse occurred. Positive numbers on the scale thus indicate a valence toward self-direction.

12. Since simultaneous controls for both current and original location amount to controls for mobility itself, one has to be removed from the list of independent variables for this analysis; current location (both region and size of place) has been deleted.

13. This does not imply that Italians and WASPs are similar in all ways. For one, they differ in their political party allegiances, with Italians notably more tied to the Democratic Party. But the crucial point is that they are similar on many traits bearing on the family-centered ethos. (For more details and discussion, see Alba, 1985.)

14. The 1980 Census yields a somewhat lower estimate of the percentage of Italians with mixed ancestry, 43.5 (versus 48.0) and presumably will show lower rates of mixed ancestry in younger cohorts when tables of ancestry by age become available. Nevertheless, there appears to be good reason to give greater credence to the Current Population Surveys (CPS) rather than the decennial Census in this case. The markedly lower estimates of mixed ancestry in general in the Census suggest that ancestry responses were more cursory to the Census's mail survey than to the face-to-face interviewing of the CPS (for further discussion of the differences between the two, see U.S. Bureau of the Census, 1983: 4–5).

REFERENCES

Alba, Richard. 1976. "Social assimilation among American Catholic national-origin groups," *American Sociological Review* 41 (December): 1030–1046.

———. 1981. "The twilight of ethnicity among American Catholics of European ancestry," *The Annals* 454 (March): 86–97.

———. 1985. *Italian Americans: Into the Twilight of Ethnicity*. Englewood Cliffs, NJ: Prentice-Hall.

Alba, Richard, and Mitchell Chamlin. 1983. "A preliminary examination of ethnic identification among whites," *American Sociological Review* 48 (April): 240–247.

Alba, Richard, and Reid Golden. 1984. "Patterns of ethnic marriage in the United States." Paper presented at the annual meetings of the American Sociological Association, Boston.

Alba, Richard, and Ronald Kessler. 1979. "Patterns of interethnic marriage among American Catholics," *Social Forces* 57 (June): 1124–1140.

Banfield, Robert. 1958. *The Moral Basis of a Backward Society*. New York: The Free Press.

Barth, Fredrik. 1969. "Introduction," in Fredrik Barth (ed.), *Ethnic Groups and Boundaries*. Boston: Little, Brown, pp. 9–38.

Berry, Brian, and John Kasarda. 1977. *Contemporary Urban Ecology*. New York: Macmillan.

Blau, Peter. 1977. *Inequality and Heterogeneity: A Primitive Theory of Social Structure*. New York: The Free Press.

Blauner, Robert. 1972. *Racial Oppression in America*. New York: Harper & Row.

Blum, Hohn Morton. 1976. *V Was for Victory: Politics and American Culture During World War II*. New York: Harcourt Brace Jovanovich.

Breton, Raymond. 1964. "Institutional completeness of ethnic communities and the personal relations of immigrants," *American Journal of Sociology* 70 (July): 193–205.

Caroli, Betty Boyd. 1973. *Italian Repatriation from the United States 1900–1914*. Staten Island, NY: Center for Migration Studies.

Chapman, Charlotte Gower. 1971. *Milocca: A Sicilian Village*. Cambridge, MA: Schenkman.

Child, Irvin. 1943. *Italian or American? Second Generation in Conflict*. New Haven, CT: Yale University Press.

Cohen, Steven. 1983. *American Modernity and Jewish Identity*. New York and London: Tavistock.

Covello, Leonard. 1972. *The Social Background of the Italo-American School Child*. Totowa: Rowman & Littlefield.

Craigie, William, and James Hulbert. 1940. *A Dictionary of American English on Historical Principles*, vol. II. Chicago: University of Chicago Press.

Crispino, James. 1980. *The Assimilation of Ethnic Groups: The Italian Case*. Staten Island, NY: Center for Migration Studies.

Davis, James, Tom Smith, and C. Bruce Stephenson. 1980. *General Social Surveys, 1972–1980: Cumulative Codebook*. Chicago: National Opinion Research Center (NORC).

Farley, Reynolds. 1985. "Recent changes in the social and economic status of blacks: Three steps forward and two back," *Ethnic and Racial Studies* (January): 4–28.

Femminella, Frank, and Jill Quadagno. 1976. "The Italian American family," in Charles Mindel and Robert Habenstein (eds.), *Ethnic Families in America: Patterns and Variations*. New York: Elsevier.

Foerster, Robert. 1924. *The Italian Emigration of Our Times*. Cambridge, MA: Harvard University Press.

Gambino, Richard. 1974. *Blood of My Blood*. Garden City, NY: Doubleday.

Gans, Herbert. 1962. *The Urban Villagers: Group and Class in the Life of Italian-Americans*. New York: The Free Press.

———. 1979. "Symbolic ethnicity: The future of ethnic groups and cultures in America," *Ethnic and Racial Studies* 2 (January): 1–20.

Glazer, Nathan, and Daniel Moynihan. 1970. *Beyond the Melting Pot*, rev. ed. Cambridge, MA: MIT Press.

Gordon, Milton. 1964. *Assimilation in American Life*. New York: Oxford University Press.

Greeley, Andrew. 1971. *Why Can't They Be Like Us?* New York: Dutton.

———. 1974. *Ethnicity in the United States: A Preliminary Reconnaissance*. New York: Wiley.

———. 1977. *The American Catholic: A Social Portrait*. New York: Basic Books.

Greeley, Andrew, and William McCready. 1975. "The transmission of cultural heritages: The case of the Irish and the Italians," in Nathan Glazer and Daniel Moynihan (eds.), *Ethnicity: Theory and Experience*. Cambridge, MA: Harvard University Press, pp. 209–235.

Hechter, Michael. 1978. "Group formation and the cultural division of labor," *American Journal of Sociology* 84 (September): 293–318.

Heer, David. 1980. "Intermarriage," in Stephan Thernstrom, Ann Orlov, and Oscar Handlin (eds.), *Harvard Encyclopedia of American Ethnic Groups*. Cambridge, MA: Harvard University Press.

Higham, John. 1970. *Strangers in the Land: Patterns of American Nativism 1860–1925*. New York: Atheneum.

Johnson, Colleen Leahy. 1982. "Sibling solidarity: Its origin and functioning in Italian-American families," *Journal of Marriage and the Family* (February): 155–167.

Kessner, Thomas. 1977. *The Golden Door: Italian and Jewish Immigrant Mobility in New York City 1880–1915*. New York: Oxford University Press.

Kohn, Melvin. 1976. "Social class and parental values: Another confirmation of the relationship," *American Sociological Review* 41 (June): 538–545.

Lieberson, Stanley. 1963. *Ethnic Patterns in American Cities*. New York: The Free Press.

———. 1980. *A Piece of the Pie: Blacks and White Immigrants since 1880*. Berkeley: University of California Press.

Mangione, Jerre. 1981. *Mount Allegro: A Memoir of Italian American Life*. New York: Columbia University Press.

Mencken, H. L. 1963. *The American Language*, abridged ed. New York: Knopf.

Merton, Robert. 1941. "Intermarriage and the social structure: Fact and theory," *Psychiatry* 4 (August): 361–374.

Miller, Herman P. 1971. *Rich Man, Poor Man*. New York: Thomas Y. Crowell.

Montero, Darrel. 1981. "The Japanese Americans: Changing patterns of assimilation over three generations," *American Sociological Review* 46 (December): 829–839.

National Opinion Research Center (NORC). *1975–80 General Social Surveys*. University of Chicago. Tabulation by author.

Newman, William M. 1973. *American Pluralism: A Study of Minority Groups and Social Theory*. New York: Harper & Row.

Novak, Michael. 1972. *The Rise of the Unmeltable Ethnics*. New York: Macmillan.

Panunzio, Constantine. 1928. *The Soul of an Immigrant*. New York.

Polenberg, Richard. 1980. *One Nation Divisible: Class, Race, and Ethnicity in the United States*. New York: Viking.

Rosen, Bernard. 1959. "Race, ethnicity, and the achievement syndrome," *American Sociological Review* 24 (February): 47–60.

Schneider, Jane, and Peter Schneider. 1976. *Culture and Political Economy in Western Sicily*. New York: Academic Press.

Schooler, Carmi. 1976. "Serfdom's legacy: An ethnic continuum," *American Journal of Sociology* 81 (May): 1265–1286.

Sori, Ercole. 1979. *L'Emigrazione italiana dall' Unita alla seconda guerra mondiale*. Bologna: Il Mulino.

Stanback, Thomas, and Richard Knight. 1970. *The Metropolitan Economy*. New York: Columbia University Press.

Steinberg, Stephen. 1982. *The Ethnic Myth: Race, Ethnicity, and Class in America*. Boston: Beacon Press.

Trow, Martin. 1961. "The second transformation of American secondary education," *International Journal of Comparative Sociology* 2: 144–166.

U.S. Bureau of the Census. 1973. *1970 Census of the Population, Volume I, Characteristics of the Population*. Washington, DC: U.S. Government Printing Office.

———. 1975. *Historical Statistics of the United States, Colonial Times to 1970*, Bicentennial edition, Part 1. Washington, DC: U.S. Government Printing Office.

———. 1982. "Ancestry and language in the United States: November 1979," *Current Population Report*, Special Studies, Series P–23, no. 116. Washington, DC: U.S. Government Printing Office.

———. 1983. *1980 Census of the Population, Ancestry of the Population by State: 1980, Supplementary Report*. Washington, DC: Government Printing Office.

U.S. Senate. 1911. *Reports of the Immigration Commission: Dictionary of Races or Peoples*. Washington, DC: U.S. Government Printing Office.

Vecoli, Rudolph J. 1978. "The coming of age of the Italian Americans," *Ethnicity* 5 (June): 119–147.

Ware, Caroline. 1935. *Greenwich Village, 1920–1930*. Boston: Houghton Mifflin.

Whyte, William Foote. 1955. *Street Corner Society*, 2d ed. Chicago: University of Chicago Press.

Woodrum, Eric. 1981. "An assessment of Japanese American assimilation, pluralism, and subordination," *American Journal of Sociology* 87 (July): 157–169.

Yancey, William, Eugene Ericksen, and Richard Juliani. 1976. "Emergent ethnicity: A review and a reformulation," *American Sociological Review* 41 (June): 391–403.

Yans-McLaughlin, Virginia. 1977. *Family and Community: Italian Immigrants in Buffalo 1880–1930*. Urbana: University of Illinois Press.

4

ASIANS, BLACKS, HISPANICS, AMERINDS: CONFRONTING VESTIGES OF SLAVERY

Stanford M. Lyman

An analytical as well as practical separation of the situations, rights, opportunities, privileges, and immunities of blacks on the one hand and immigrants on the other has been part of American social thought at least since 1782, when Hector St. Jean de Crèvecoeur defined "the American" as an amalgam of the several European strains together with those of the indigenous Indians but confined mention of the Africans in the new nation to a solicitous concern for their slave status.[1] The same distinction found its way into William Wells Brown's *Clotel* (1853), the first novel written by an African American, when the author contrasted the deadly fate that overtook his eponymous heroine, a fugitive slave and the illegitimate daughter of Thomas Jefferson, with the initial welcome and social acceptance that would have been hers had she been a white woman in flight from Europe's despotisms.[2] The amendments added to the Constitution in the five years following the Union victory in the Civil War intentionally if only by implication continued the distinction not only by abolishing slavery but also by granting citizenship specifically to persons of African descent and seeking to remove from them the entire complex of "badges," "incidents," and

This chapter was presented at the Eastern Sociological Society annual meetings, Boston, May 1, 1987.

"indicia" of their two centuries of involuntary servitude. Although the first quarter century of the Amendments' life witnessed the Supreme Court's constriction of the applicable scope of the Amendments to a prohibition on Negro reenslavement,[3] and though the Court permitted the doctrine of separate-but-equal to rule with respect to virtually all "colored"-white institutional arrangements from 1896[4] to 1954,[5] a more recent Court in 1968 reaffirmed the original broader meaning and extended the application of the Amendments[6] and their supportive legislation. Moreover, Congress has seen fit to legislate a requirement of affirmative action affecting not only the equal opportunities of blacks but also those of certain other minorities.[7]

However, the groups now eligible for the benefits that affirmative action programs confer cut across the old division separating blacks from immigrants and include descendants of nonwhite and non-Anglo members of the latter while excluding the others. Opponents of affirmative action have called the new class of eligibles into question, referring to it as an instantiation of "reverse discrimination."[8] Defenders of the new approach to equality have had to search out a justification for the new division and show it to be within the purview of reason and the Constitution.[9]

This chapter is directed toward confirming the legal rectitude of the new division and redeeming it from the charge of reverse discrimination. Substantively, this is a study in the historical sociology of American constitutional law; methodologically, it proceeds in accordance with an approach to classificatory matters that arose originally from Emile Durkheim's and Marcel Mauss's formulation,[10] has moved through that of Herbert Blumer and the symbolic interactionists,[11] and has been combined for purposes of the present investigation with that employed in conventionalized jurisprudential classificational procedure.[12]

Recently litigated affirmative action programs have extended their benefits not only to blacks but also to certain nonwhite and non-Anglo peoples. Although the industrial craft training program sustained by the Supreme Court in *Weber v. Kaiser* (1979) established its special school exclusively for blacks, the category of persons eligible for eighteen reserved seats in the medical school under the University of California at Davis's constitu-

tionally unsuccessful experiment in affirmative action embraced
self-designated members of such "disadvantaged minority
groups" as blacks, Chicanos, Asians, and American Indians; the
ethnoracial limitation on layoffs concluded in the judicially dis-
approved collective bargaining agreement signed by the Jackson,
Michigan, Board of Education, which protected black, American
Indian, Oriental, and Hispanic teachers; the Court-approved
consent decree entered into by the City of Cleveland with respect
to the hiring and promotion of firefighters required special affirmative action procedures with respect to black and Hispanic
male and female firefighters; and a New York City sheet metal
workers' union local was ordered to institute a percentage admissions plan positively affecting the job chances of blacks and
Hispanics. Common to almost all these plans—both those that
meet and those that fail the test of judicial scrutiny—is a classification of eligibles that includes nonwhite, non-Anglo peoples
and by implication excludes members of white Anglo and European descent groups.

Critics of affirmative action insist that these programs are instances of reverse discrimination in that they grant educational
privileges and/or open up job and career opportunities to one
group but deny these same privileges and opportunities to all
those not included in the beneficial plan. Because they believe
that advantages in education and opportunities for employment
should be granted in accordance with a strictly individualized
meritocratic policy, the most consistent critics of affirmative action should oppose any program that modifies such an ideal.
However, neither the Supreme Court, the federal government,
nor all enemies of affirmative action engages in advocacy for an
unmodified meritocracy. Racial classifications have been held to
be suspect by the Supreme Court but not absolutely forbidden
to the accomplishment of an otherwise lawful public purpose.[13]
In a case decided before he retired from the bench, Chief Justice
Warren Burger pointed out that although the Court must "recognize the need for careful judicial evaluation to assure that any
congressional program that employs racial or ethnic criteria to
accomplish the objective of remedying the present effects of past
discrimination is narrowly tailored to the achievement of that
goal . . . , we reject the contention that in the remedial context

the Congress must act in a wholly 'color-blind' fashion."[14] By the same token, both state and federal governments have enacted such Court-sustained laws as those granting a monopoly on becoming Mississippi River pilots to the sons of river pilots;[15] a restriction on being a female bar employee unless one is the wife or daughter of the bar owner;[16] a subsidy to attend college or university and to gain unearned points on a Civil Service Examination to all those who served in the military during World War II and the Korean and Vietnam wars, while excluding those who served the government in a nonmilitary capacity during the same wars.

Finally, it should be noted that one of the currently most active opponents of affirmative action, Nathan Glazer, from the very beginning of his protests on the matter denied that the United States had ever existed except in its own dreamy-eyed ideology about itself as a single "American community . . . in [which] . . . heritage, ethnicity, religion, [and] race are only incidental and accidental personal characteristics." Glazer insists that "liberal principles—[including] . . . the newer ones arguing the democracy of merit—. . . are being increasingly accepted by everyone . . . nowadays under the pressures of a technological world," but that the pressure exerted by blacks to break down ethnocultural barriers to their own education, employment, and economic opportunity threatens "institutions which are the true seats of Jewish exclusiveness—the Jewish business, for example, the Jewish union, or the Jewish (or largely Jewish) neighborhood and school."[17] Hence, it can be concluded that a proposal to confer special privileges or particular immunities upon racial or ethnic sodalities does not in and of itself constitute a *prima facie* violation of the pattern of American educational, residential, occupational organization; nor does every legislated ethnic, racial, or gender classification violate the guaranty of equal protections of the law that the Constitution provides for each person in the United States.

"It is clear," observes the constitutional scholar Jacobus ten Broek, "that the demand for equal protection cannot be a demand that laws apply universally to all persons." Legislatures, when they act to eliminate an evil practice or to promote some aspect of the public welfare, "must impose special burdens upon, or grant special benefits to, special groups or classes of individuals."[18] Legislatures, then, are the architects engaged in a legal and equitable construction and reconstruction of the public reality. In so doing, they ideally pursue the public interest in freedom, justice, and equality by so distributing the burdens and benefits of civil life in America that none shall be denied or deprived of the rights and opportunities that flow therefrom. The classifications made by a legislature, or by any agency charged with the task of assuring a just distribution of items of positive value, are not "natural" nor must they necessarily be congruent with any categorizations or groupings that exist in the world outside of lawful legislative intent. Rather, a legislative classification meets the test of equal protections constitutionality when it is made in furtherance of a permissible public purpose and when, "within the sphere of its operation, it affects alike all persons similarly situated"[19] and none who are not.[20] Hence, the classifications made by affirmative action proposals can be tested. They can be evaluated with respect to whether or not they serve a lawful public purpose in a manner that embraces only those who deserve the benefits it seeks to confer.

As a first step in this examination, the public purpose that affirmative action programs serve must be determined. Generally, they are alleged to remedy past discriminations, but this is not sufficient to clarify the propriety of their classificatory limitations, prescribe classificatory exactitude, or even to ensure their lawful character. Here, it is suggested that these programs constitute a continuation of the mandate imposed on the post–Civil War national and state governments to remove the "badges," "incidents," and "indicia" of slavery from all those affected by these.[21] Race discrimination against the emancipated blacks was at first recognized as the most significant of the badges of slavery in that it reinforced and gave manifest expression to the allegation that African Americans belonged to an inferior caste of human beings. However, in the first three decades that followed adoption of the Thirteenth, Fourteenth, and Fifteenth Amendments to the Constitution, the Supreme Court restricted the meaning, scope, and application of their promise to a simple prohibition on reenslavement and involuntary servitude.[22] Judge Loren Miller summarized the Supreme Court's role in this constriction of the freedmen's rights:

In the *Slaughter-house Cases*, it restored the *Dred Scott* doctrine that there are two categories of citizenship, national and state, and gutted the privileges and immunities clause of the fourteenth amendment of all meaning. In *United States v. Cruikshank*, it restored control of civil rights to the states. In *United States v. Reese*, it severely restricted the scope and reach of the fifteenth amendment. In the *Civil Rights Cases*, it further cabined the meaning of the fourteenth amendment with its ruling that Congress could not proscribe an individual's discriminatory conduct. In *Virginia v. Rives*, it validated the indictments of all-white juries in the absence of specific objections and proof by a Negro defendant of systematic and purposeful racial exclusion, and thus it set up a rule which allowed extensive discrimination in jury selection. In *William v. Mississippi*, and later in *Giles v. Harris* and *Giles v. Teasley*, it gave its blessing to state constitutional and statutory provisions deliberately and professedly designed to circumscribe the franchise. In *Plessy v. Ferguson*, it approved a state's racial classification, undertaken to establish the separate-but-equal rule in the use of state facilities or public utilities. In *Berea College v. Kentucky*, it approved state statutes proscribing interracial association for innocent purposes.[23]

Throughout the era of constriction, at least one dissenting judicial voice was raised in behalf of the original intent and range of application of the postwar amendments. In 1883, Justice John Marshall Harlan reminded his colleagues that their majority decision in the Civil Rights Cases would permit race "discrimination [to be] practiced by corporations and individuals in the exercise of their public or quasi public functions," and he asserted that such discrimination was "a badge of servitude the imposition of which Congress may prevent under its power, by appropriate legislation, to enforce the Thirteenth Amendment."[24] Thirteen years later, Harlan dissented from the Court's majority decision upholding Louisiana's law requiring racially separate-but-equal coaches for passengers on interstate railroads, pointing out that the "arbitrary separation of citizens, on the basis of race, while they are on a public highway, is a badge of servitude wholly inconsistent with the civil freedom and the equality before the law established by the Constitution."[25] He concluded that if other states were to enact similar segregative legislation, even though the institution of slavery had disappeared, "there would remain a power in the states, by sinister legislation, to interfere with the full enjoyment of the blessings of freedom; to regulate civil rights, common to all citizens, upon the basis of race; and to place in a condition of legal inferiority a large body of American citizens, now constituting a part of the political community called the people of the United States."[26] Moreover, Harlan was of the opinion that the Amendments not only commanded the government to protect the freedmen and women from all of the proactive vestiges of slavery, but that it had an affirmative obligation to do so. In his dissent in the Civil Rights Cases, he rebuked the Court's majority for suggesting that the emancipated blacks had been "the special favorite of the laws," pointing out that in their case it had been deemed proper not merely " 'to help the feeble up, but to support him after,' " but observing that at "every step, in this direction, the nation has been confronted with class tyranny."[27]

A return to something approximating Harlan's broader scope of the Amendments did not occur until after 1954, the year the Warren Court declared public school segregation inconsistent with the equal protections of the law guaranteed by the Fourteenth Amendment.[28] Subsequent orders to desegregate schools with all deliberate speed led to reconsideration of the worthiness, rectitude, and constitutionality of compensatory policies that might redress past inequities. "The critical question," wrote Judge Miller in 1966, "is whether the color-blind constitution which equalitarians have always demanded will tolerate such compensatory measures." Reminding his readers that the Reconstruction Congress had had "no constitutional qualms about enactment of remedial legislation such as the Freedmen's Bureau Acts, which were designed to assist Negroes and newly freed slaves," Miller supposed that "compensatory legislation designed to benefit Negroes as a class is constitutionally permissible."[29] Here, it should be noted, the implication was that the affirmative benefits were to be conferred upon the descendants of the African-American slaves insofar as they were present-day victims of the still operative badges of slavery.

That the mandate to remove the vestiges of slavery was still constitutionally viable was asserted by the Supreme Court in 1968. In a decision upholding a congressional statute (42 U.S.C. 1982) requiring that, "All citizens of the United States shall have the same right, in every State and Territory, as is enjoyed by white citizens thereof to inherit, purchase, lease, sell, hold, and convey real and personal property," the Court held the law to be a valid exercise of Congress's power to implement the full intent of the Thirteenth Amendment. That Court, citing the speech of Illinois Senator Lyman Trumbull, who had chaired the Judiciary Committee that had brought the Thirteenth Amendment to the Senate floor in 1864, pointed out that "Congress has the power under the Thirteenth Amendment rationally to determine what are the badges and the incidents of slavery and the authority to translate that determination into effective legislation."[30] Race discrimination against blacks was held to be a badge of slavery, and Congress was recognized to be serving a valid public interest in enacting laws that forbade it. Three years later,[31] the Supreme Court held, in the words of Herbert Hill, "that the use of tests by employers to make hiring and promotion decisions violates Title VII [of the Civil Rights Act of 1964] when such tests have no relationship to successful job performance and operate to disqualify blacks at a substantially higher rate than white applicants."[32] And even when, in 1976, the Court refused to invalidate a verbal ability, vocabulary, and reading comprehension test for police officers in Washington, DC that resulted in disqualifying a high proportion of black applicants, it still recognized that the "central purpose of the Equal Protection Clause of the Fourteenth Amendment is the prevention of official conduct discriminating on the basis of race" and went on to observe that even when a disriminatory intent is not written into the text of a law, "an invidious discriminatory purpose may often be inferred from the totality of the relevant facts."[33]

That neither the Congress nor the judiciary is required to be color-blind in relieving blacks from the heritage of slavery and the discriminatory vestiges thereof is clear from the record of Supreme Court decisions. The more pressing question—the one that informs the charge of reverse discrimination against many affirmative action programs—is whether the benefits of such remedial programs may be reasonably and constitutionally extended to include Asians, Hispanics, and Amerinds at the same time that they are refused to white anglo descendants of European immigrants. The matter depends on whether the bar of inclusion-exclusion meets the test of reasonable relationship to the valid public purpose enunciated above.

In order to meet this requirement it must be shown that the racial and ethnic discriminations suffered by Asians, Hispanics, and Indians are vestiges of the system of black slavery, while those encountered by European immigrants and their American-born descent groups stem from some other source or sources. Should it be shown that there are dual trajectories of racial and ethnic discrimination, that one of them arose out of the imposition of a racially based system of involuntary servitude while the other stemmed from one or several aspects of a particularized and selective xenophobia, then it would follow that legislative programs designed to eradicate the badges of slavery should embrace all those persons and groups who are properly shown to have been victimized by the heritage of bondage and none who have not. Although much work has been done to compare the conditions of work and life of immigrants with those of blacks, little effort has been made to see whether the ancillary and vestigial effects of slavery had a "horizontal" as well as a temporal dimension, that is, whether they reached out to engulf select groups among the immigrant peoples and tarred them as well as the freedmen and women with the brush of inferiorization. The following discussion suggests a body of evidence supporting this hypothesis and invites further research on the topic.

PLURALIZED VERSUS PLURAL SOCIETIES

In his important reconceptualization of the beginnings of the race question in America, Benjamin Ringer offers implicit support for the rightful categorization of blacks, Asians, and Hispanics as peoples deserving the benefits of affirmative action. He contends:

the thirteen colonies created two different kinds of pluralized societies.
... One kind, a pluralistic society, reflected the instability and fluidity
that operated within white colonist America. The other kind, a plural
society, reflected the stabilized structure of repression that had come
to characterize relations between black and white by the end of the
colonial period. There seems to be no doubt that one version was built
on the back of the enslaved black.[34]

If this thesis is accepted, then it would seem to follow that the
inferiorization of blacks arose out of their enslavement and that,
as a vestige of slavery, that inferiorization is the principal element of their condition to be eradicated by any legislative action
taken to implement the Thirteenth Amendment. However, as
Ringer seems to suggest, the pattern of racially repressive duality
first formulated in slavocratic America was not exorcised from
the body politic after the Emancipation but was instead remod-
eled and extended to include political, social, and economic discriminations against Asians and Hispanics as well as the newly
freed Negroes.[35] Although Ringer's thesis includes, *inter alia*, a
defense of affirmative action programs against the claim by Nathan Glazer, Thomas Sowell, and others that they institution-
alize "reverse discrimination," he does not proceed to an
analysis or a direct justification of the classificatory dichotomy
that these programs entail.

With respect to the comparability of black and white immigrant situations since 1880, Stanley Lieberson has recently provided evidence that might be employed to justify exclusion of
the latter group from affirmative action remediation:

The situation for new Europeans in the United States, bad as it may
have been, was not as bad as that experienced by blacks at the same
time. Witness, for example, the differences in the disposition to ban
openly blacks from unions at the turn of the century ..., the greater
concentration of blacks in 1990 in service occupations and their smaller
number in manufacturing and mechanical jobs ..., the higher black
death rates in the North ..., and even the greater segregation of blacks
with respect to the avenues of eminence open to them. ... It is a serious
mistake to underestimate how far the new Europeans have come in the
nation and how hard it all was, but it is equally erroneous to assume
that the obstacles were as great as those faced by blacks or that the
starting point was the same.[36]

Moreover, Lieberson notes the distinctive differences in federal immigration restriction and in white Anglo Americans' rank order of desirability with respect to Europeans on the one hand and blacks and nonwhite peoples from Asia on the other: "Attitudinal surveys administered in the 1920s confirm the notion that the groups were implicitly ranked on a continuum of inferiority. . . . In a variety of surveys, the American population ranked Northwestern Europeans highest, then the South-Central-Eastern Europeans, in turn the Japanese and Chinese, and finally blacks."[37] Lieberson explains the relatively greater accomplishments of Asian Americans in the employment and educational sectors by referring to the reduction in their "threat" imagery (a reduction that occurred after their immigration to the United States was cut off), to their concentration in certain regions of the United States where their mutual aid practices might shield them from the worst aspects of American racism, and to their discovery of and entrance into certain narrow occupational niches through which they might achieve a modest economic advance.[38] Lieberson has little to say about Hispanics in America, but he does note that the extraordinarily high rate of illiteracy recorded in 1920 for "native whites" of "foreign parentage" in the west–south central region of the United States "reflects the sizable numbers of second-generation Mexicans present"[39] and projects, for the year 1960, a measure of the ratio of a people's nonfarm workforce engaged in more desirable craft occupations in relation to those in semiskilled jobs in which native whites of native parentage rank highest (.97); second-generation white groups of European parentage never fall below—and usually score several points above—that of Greek Americans (.64); and second-generation Mexicans score .55, with only blacks (.38) falling below them.

Chinese

There is evidence to suggest that Asians were regarded as surrogates for blacks and as likely candidates for a process of inferiorization similar to that imposed on the latter both before and after Emancipation. Henry Hughes (1829–1862), America's first sociologist, proposed to the legislature of Mississippi in 1856 that Chinese might be imported into that state from Cuba and then subjected to enslavement—after their inferiority had been ascertained scientifically.[40] In the first decade after slavery had been abolished, the importation of Chinese contract workers to replace the freedmen was the objective of the nefarious and unsuccessful "Koopmanschap incident" in Louisiana.[41] However, Southern plantation owners, eager "to rid themselves of their dependence on blacks," turned to the Chinese.[42] In one not unusual example, a Mrs. Leigh of Georgia "entered into a scheme to employ Chinese workers on McIntosh plantations. As a part of this plan, A. S. Barnwell brought in thirty coolies to work General's Island."[43] More indicative of the treatment of Chinese as substitutes for degraded blacks was their employment as night-shift contract laborers in the cotton mills set up inside the Louisiana State Penitentiary, which had been leased to Samuel L. James and Company as an industrial enterprise.[44] Chinese in the south worked as railroad hands, fishermen,[45] and, all too often to suit the purposes of their importers, set themselves up as independent storekeepers;[46] but they were originally thought to be slave replacements on sugar, tobacco, and cotton plantations. Moreover, a veritable degradation ceremony with respect to Chinese workers was conducted by key members of the United States Senate in 1876, who, even when faced with testimony that contradicted their prejudicial presuppositions, persisted in linking Chinese to Negroes and regarding both as a menace to white laboring interests and to the civilization of the United States.[47] The testimony of Henry George, a forerunner of certain theories about progress and poverty that are still in vogue in some parts of the United States,[48] is instructive in regard to the comparison of Chinese with blacks on the one hand and southern and eastern Europeans on the other:

Q. You think that, like the negro, the Chinese are incapable of attaining a high state of civilization?

A. They are incapable of attaining the state of civilization the Caucasian is capable of.

Q. You would make the same objection to the introduction of the negro to civilization as to the introduction of the Chinese on that ground.

A. I would have the same objection to the introduction of the negro as to the importation of the Chinese.[49]

Q. Has this influx of Chinese tended to degrade the dignity of labor?

A. Undoubtedly.

Q. Has it had a tendency to bring white labor into the same repute that slavery did in the Southern States?

A. I think its ultimate effects are precisely the same upon the white race as slavery.[50]

Q. Why is the Italian immigration preferable to the Chinese?

A. They are of a different race. The Italians are of the same stock as we are, and have come to their present pitch by a slow course of development for thousands of years.

Q. They are a higher civilization?

A. Undoubtedly.

Q. Do you think the same objection would apply to any lower civilization as to the Chinese?

A. Undoubtedly.[51]

Q. [D]o the Italians assimilate with us and become part and portion of our body-politic?

A. Undoubtedly.

Q. Do they become citizens and take upon themselves the duties of citizens?

A. Undoubtedly.

Q. And so of the Irish, the Germans, and all others of the European family?

A. Yes, sir.

Q. In time do they so assimilate with us that they are American?

A. Yes, sir.

Q. We are all of that stock, are we not?

A. Yes, sir.[52]

Q. Do you think, as a race, they [that is, the Chinese] would make fit citizens?

A. O, no; I have not the slightest comprehension that they would; it is totally foreign to their ideas.

Q. You do not think they could be made such?

A. O, no.

Q. You think it would be an injury to our civilization to incorporate them with us?

A. It would be utterly destructive.[53]

For those post-Emancipation leaders concerned with establishing an agricultural and industrial labor force, enhancing American civilization, and regenerating the citizenry, Europeans were welcome as assimilatable, while the Chinese were regarded as a racially and culturally inferior, unfairly competitive, and civically dangerous people—a people not even fit for citizenship and the franchise that had been granted to blacks by the Fifteenth Amendment.

Japanese

The Japanese were perceived as a people deserving the kinds of treatment meted out to the exslaves, the Chinese, and the American Indians; this indicates not only their separation from European immigrants in the policies, minds, and hearts of majority group Americans but also their deserving of a place among the beneficiaries of affirmative action. Held to be neither "free white persons" nor "persons of African descent," Japanese immigrants, like the Chinese, were assigned to an ignominious legal status: "aliens ineligible to citizenship in the United States." One Japanese immigrant, aspiring to United States citizenship, unsuccessfully petitioned the Supreme Court to declare his people to be Caucasians.[54] A few years earlier, Robert E. Park, the preeminent sociologist of race and ethnic relations in the United States, issued a doleful prophecy: "The Japanese, like the Negro, is condemned to remain among us an abstraction, a symbol, and a symbol not merely of his own race, but of the Orient and of that vague, ill-defined menace we sometimes refer to as the 'yellow peril.' "[55]

It was in one of his fulminations against the Chinese that

Henry George proposed the policy later used in an attempt to evict the Japanese from their principal occupational niche, the family farm: "Root the white race in the soil," George had exhorted his listeners, "and all the millions of Asia cannot dispossess it."[56] The Chinese had been driven out of California's agricultural fields by a series of strikes in the late 1870s and 1880s. The Japanese smallholder was subjected to the privations of California's and thirteen other states' alien land laws which—though enacted too late to be fully effective—sought to drive the Japanese off the land.[57] When, early in the twentieth century, Japanese farmers pioneered the production of tropical fruits in Florida, they were classed as a people similar in habits to the freedmen and were subjected to many of the same kinds of prejudices.[58] However, Japanese suffered their most severe material and moral injuries in the years 1942–1945, when 120,000 Americans of Japanese descent, 65 percent of whom were citizens of the United States, were imprisoned on wastelands in specially constructed prison camps and guarded by American military personnel—all of this done without a criminal charge, a presumption of innocence, or a court trial.[59] At the present time, Japanese American survivors of the wartime policy are awaiting receipt of the redress payments recommended by President Ford's special commission on their treatment during World War II[60] and hailing the outcome of the cases mounted in the mid–1980s to reverse the Supreme Court decisions of 1943 and 1944 that justified the curfew, evacuation, and imprisonment.[61]

It should be noted that during the course of the congressional hearings held in February 1942, both the mayor of Los Angeles and a spokesman for California's Tulare County proposed that Japanese Americans be forcibly moved to uninhabited American Indian reservations on the California-Arizona border.[62] The sequestration of American-born Japanese was regarded as even more important than the removal of alien Japanese because, according to California Attorney-General Earl Warren, some of the former (i.e., the *Kibei*) had attended school in Japan and had become indoctrinated with a "religious instruction which ties up their religion with their Emperor" and because the loyalty of the American-educated *Nisei* could not be established by any known means. However, it is to be noted that Warren and others believed that the loyalty of German and Italian aliens could easily be established.[63]

Hispanics

Hispanic peoples in America belong to a civilizational body that embraces all those lands and peoples affected by the imperialist phase of the Spanish seaborne empire. For practical purposes, however, the Hispanic groups deemed eligible for affirmative action in the United States are of Mexican and Puerto Rican descent. Mexican and Mexican-American peoples of California and the southwest found that their status hung precariously between that of blacks and anglos while their economic condition was marked by difficult-to-dislodge but illegal practices of peonage or by migratory labor in California's Confederate-derived system of agribusiness. All too often, their educational opportunities were restricted through segregated and inferior school systems. Deemed to be slightly higher on the social scale than blacks, Mexican Americans found themselves subjected to the group positioning that is characteristic of slavery's legacy of American race prejudice.[64]

Puerto Ricans, Mexicans, and American Indians have had their various positions in the American racial order regulated by law. Whereas Mexican residents in the ceded territories had one year to decide whether or not to opt for American citizenship,[65] Puerto Ricans and American Indians found their own anomalous civic statuses to be governed by novel additions to international law. In the case of Puerto Rico, the Foraker Act of 1900 established the newly conquered island community as an unincorporated territory whose denizens had no clear right to U.S. citizenship. As part of its justification for imposing this unusual status, Senatorial Report number 249 held the Puerto Ricans to be a "people of wholly different character, illiterate, and unacquainted with our institutions, and incapable of exercising the rights and privileges guaranteed by the Constitution." Because of their condition, the Report concluded that it "would be competent for Congress to withhold from such people the operation of the Constitution and the laws of the United States . . . [and to] govern the people thereof as their situation and the necessities of their case might seem to require."[66] That the minds of at least some of the Congressmen were turned toward comparing the Puerto Ricans and the Filipinos (whose homeland was also acquired as a result of the Spanish-American War) with the freedmen and the Chinese is indicated in this statement from the Democratic congressman from Kentucky: "We are trying to keep out the Chinese with one hand, and now you are proposing to make Territories of the United States out of Puerto Rico and the Philippine Islands, and thereby open wide the door by which the negroes [sic] and Asiatics can pour like the locusts of Egypt into this country."[67] Although the rights, privileges, and immunities of citizenship were eventually granted to Puerto Ricans and a number of their people entered into the middle classes, an even larger number found themselves members of a servile under-class, employed on white-Anglo-dominated sugar plantations on the island or crowded into the poverty-stricken slums of Spanish Harlem, an ethnoracial ghetto in New York City. All too often considered to be Negroes, Puerto Ricans in effect bore the stigma of bondage—the badge of inferiority—that had arisen in the age and through the institutionalization of black slavery.

Amerinds

Amerinds (or American Indians) owe their unusual status to their identification as Asians,[68] their selection for and resistance to enslavement, and their subsequent degradation as members of a uniquely conceived "domestic dependent nation." In a concurrence with the paramount decision that has been decisive in determining their rights, privileges, and immunities since 1831, the Supreme Court's Associate Justice, Mr. William Johnson, was of the opinion that the Native Americans were not members of foreign states but rather of "Indian tribes—an anomaly unknown to the books that treat of States, and which the law of nations would regard as nothing more than wandering hordes, held together only by ties of blood and habit, and having neither laws or governments, beyond what is required in a savage state."[69] The opinion of the Court, delivered by Chief Justice John Marshall, held that "it may well be doubted whether those tribes which reside within the acknowledged boundaries of the

United States can, with strict accuracy, be denominated foreign nations. They may, more correctly, perhaps, be denominated domestic dependent nations. . . . Meanwhile, they are in a state of pupilage. Their relation to the United States resembles that of a ward to his guardian."[70] Having been reduced to the collective status of pupils and wards, the Indians were made to resemble the enslaved Negro, insofar as the latter, under the degrading designation of "Sambo," was held to be in a state of perpetual childhood. The conflation of "savage" with "child" completed the cycle of degradation, circumscribing the limits of free action, competitive opportunities, civil rights, and social privileges within which this people might move.

As the twenty-first century approaches, scholarly concerns might well turn to the future of the American dream—especially as that dream affects the various races already settled in the United States, the immigrants presently arriving, and those who in the future will arrive on the shores of the United States. That future in part depends on the resolution of lingering conflicts, conflicts that arose in America's misunderstood racial and ethnic past and that evoke bitter dispute today. America's present and future immigrants, despite their material, moral, cultural, and historical uniqueness, will likely be identified with ethnic or racial elements of the settled American population. They will be seen as new generations of and people deserving the prevalent attitudes and policies toward Europeans, Latin Americans, Asians, Oceanians, or Africans. These heritages are themselves matters of dispute, as are the various proposals for remedies and eligibility for redress for past discriminations. This chapter has suggested a hypothesis that might inform both research and policy with respect to this debate: that, in America, there have been two distinctive and distinguishable trajectories of discrimination, but—although I have not detailed that trajectory that affects Euro-Americans and derives from a generalized xenophobia—only one, that which descended from the badges of slavery, is remediable under the mandate that the Thirteenth Amendment to the Constitution gives to the Fourteenth and that affects its special class of eligibles. Should this thesis be accepted, affirmative action programs benefitting blacks, Asians,

Amerinds, and Hispanics would be rid of the accusation of reverse discrimination and welcomed as part of the remedy that remains to be employed in solution to this discriminatory dilemma.

Fulfillment of the American dream requires that we awaken from the American nightmare of racial and ethnic prejudice and face and act on the issues of both racism and xenophobia in the clear light of rational and scientific thought. Then the future might become brighter as the promise of American life is realized in the performance of the nation's institutions.

NOTES

1. Hector St. John de Crevecoeur, *Letters from an American Farmer* (New York: E. P. Dutton, 1957. Orig. pub. in 1782), pp. 35–82, 137, 156–168, 187–189.

2. William Wells Brown, *Clotel, Or The President's Daughter: A Narrative of Slave Life in the United States* (New York: Citadel Press, 1969. Orig. pub. in 1853), pp. 219–220.

3. Civil Rights Cases, 109 U.S. 3 (1883).

4. *Plessy vs. Ferguson*, 163 U.S. 537 (1896).

5. *Brown vs. Board of Education of Topeka*, 347 U.S. (1954).

6. *Jones vs. Alfred H. Mayer Co.*, 392 U.S. 409 (1968).

7. *Title VII of the Civil Rights Act*, 42 U.S.C. sec. 2000e et seq. (1964).

8. See, for example, Justice Scalia et al., Dissent, *Johnson vs. Transportation Agency of Santa Clara County, California, et al.*, no. 85–1129 (March 25, 1987), pp. 1–21.

9. See, for example, three works by Ronald Dworkin, *Taking Rights Seriously* (Cambridge, MA: Harvard University Press, 1978), pp. 223–239; *A Matter of Principle* (Cambridge, MA: Harvard University Press, 1985), pp. 293–334; *Law's Empire* (Cambridge, MA: The Belknap Press of Harvard University Press, 1986), pp. 355–399.

10. Emile Durkheim and Marcel Mauss, *Primitive Classification*, translated and edited by Rodney Needham (Chicago: University of Chicago Press, 1967. Orig. pub. in 1903); *Durkheim on Politics and the State*, translated by W. D. Halls, edited by Anthony Giddens (Stanford, CA: Stanford University Press, 1986), pp. 97–121.

11. Herbert Blumer, *Symbolic Interactionism: Perspective and Method* (Englewood Cliffs, NJ: Prentice-Hall, 1969), pp. 10–12. See also the discussion of affirmative action in Stanford M. Lyman and Arthur J. Vidich, *Social Order and the Public Philosophy: An Analysis and Commentary*

on the Works of Herbert Blumer (Fayetteville: University of Arkansas Press, 1988), pp. 61–91.

12. See Joseph Tussman and Jacobus ten Broek, "The Equal Protection of the Laws," *California Law Review*, XXXVII (September 1949), 341–381.

13. *Korematsu vs. United States*, 323 U.S. 214 (1944), 216.

14. *Fullilove vs. Klutznick*, 448 U.S. 448 (1980).

15. *Kotch vs. Board of River Pilot Commissioners*, 330 U.S. 552 (1947).

16. *Goesaert vs. Cleary*, 335 U.S. 464 (1948). But see *Craig vs. Boren*, 429 U.S. 190 (1976).

17. Nathan Glazer, "Negroes and Jews: The New Challenge to Pluralism," *Commentary*, XXXVIII (December 1964), 29–35. Reprinted in Nathan Glazer, *Ethnic Dilemmas, 1964–1982* (Cambridge, MA: Harvard University Press, 1983), pp. 29–43. Quotations from pp. 42 and 37, respectively.

18. Jacobus ten Broek, *Equal Under Law*, enlarged ed. (New York: Collier Books, 1965), p. 21.

19. *Yick Wo vs. Hopkins*, 118 U.S. 356 (1886).

20. Tussman and ten Broek, "The Equal Protection of the Laws," pp. 344–356.

21. See Jacobus ten Broek, "Thirteenth Amendment to the Constitution of the United States: Consummation to Abolition and Key to the Fourteenth Amendment," *California Law Review* XXXIX (June 1951), 171–203.

22. Even this proved difficult to enforce. See Sydney Brodie, "The Federally-Secured Right to be Free From Bondage," *Georgetown Law Review*, XL (March 1952), 367–398; and Harry H. Shapiro, "Involuntary Servitude: The Need for a More Flexible Approach," *Rutgers Law Review* LXV (Fall 1964), 65–85.

23. Loren Miller, "Race, Poverty, and the Law," in Jacobus ten Broek and the editors of the *California Law Review* (eds.), *The Law of the Poor* (San Francisco: Chandler Publishing Company, 1966), p. 67.

24. Dissent, Civil Rights Cases.

25. Dissent, *Plessy vs. Ferguson*, 163 U.S. 256 (1896).

26. Ibid.

27. Dissent, Civil Rights Cases.

28. *Brown v. Board of Education of Topeka*, 347 U.S. 483 (1954).

29. Miller, "Race, Poverty, and the Law," p. 81.

30. *Jones v. Alfred H. Mayer Co.*

31. *Griggs v. Duke Power Co.*, 401 U.S. 424 (1971).

32. Herbert Hill, *Black Labor and the American Legal System: Race, Work and the Law* (Madison: University of Wisconsin Press, 1985), p. 61.

33. *Washington, Mayor of Washington v. Davis*, 426 U.S. 229 (1976).

34. Benjamin Ringer, *"We the People" and Others: Duality and America's Treatment of Its Racial Minorities* (New York: Tavistock Publications, 1983), p. 80.

35. Ibid., pp. 157–1097.

36. Stanley Lieberson, *A Piece of the Pie: Blacks and White Immigrants Since 1880* (Berkeley: University of California Press, 1980), p. 383.

37. Ibid., p. 31.

38. Ibid., pp. 5–7, 30–31, 207, 365–382.

39. Ibid., p. 134.

40. See Stanford M. Lyman, "Henry Hughes and the Southern Foundation of American Sociology," in Stanford M. Lyman (ed.), *Selected Writings of Henry Hughes: Antebellum Southerner, Slavocrat, Sociologist* (Jackson: University of Mississippi, 1985), pp. 24–25.

41. See two works by Stanford M. Lyman, *The Structure of Chinese Society in Nineteenth Century America*, Ph.D. dissertation, University of California, Berkeley, 1961, pp. 399–404; and *Chinatown and Little Tokyo: Power, Conflict, and Community Among Chinese and Japanese Immigrants in America* (Millwood, NY: Associated Faculty Press, 1986), pp. 240–242. See also Gunther Barth, *Bitter Strength: A History of the Chinese in the United States, 1850–1870* (Cambridge, MA: Harvard University Press, 1964), pp. 191–197; and Lucy M. Cohen, *Chinese in the Post–Civil War South: A People Without a History* (Baton Rouge: Louisiana State University Press, 1984), pp. 67–70, 89–95, 120–123, 180–182.

42. See, for example, Michael Wayne, *The Reshaping of Plantation Society: The Natchez District, 1860–1880* (Baton Rouge: Louisiana State University Press, 1983), pp. 60–61, 68–72. See also Lyman, "Henry Hughes," pp. 51–54; and Cohen, *Chinese in the Post–Civil War South*, pp. 46–81.

43. Russell Duncan, *Freedom's Shore: Tunis Campbell and the Georgia Freedmen* (Athens: University of Georgia Press, 1986), p. 60.

44. Cohen, *Chinese in the Post–Civil War South*, pp. 93–94.

45. Roger Shugg, *Origins of Class Struggle in Louisiana: A Social History of White Farmers and Laborers During Slavery and After, 1840–1875* (Baton Rouge: Louisiana State University Press, 1972. Orig. pub. in 1939), pp. 254–255, 311–312.

46. Cohen, *Chinese in the Post–Civil War South*; James W. Loewen, *The Mississippi Chinese: Between Black and White* (Cambridge, MA: Harvard University Press, 1971), pp. 32–57; Robert Seto Quan, in collaboration with Julian B. Roebuck, *Lotus Among the Magnolias: The Mississippi Chinese* (Jackson: University Press of Mississippi, 1982), pp. 68–99.

47. United States Senate, Forty-fourth Congress, *Report of the Joint*

Special Committee to Investigate Chinese Immigration (Washington, DC: U.S. Government Printing Office, 1877), pp. 82, 289, 293–294, 942, 953–956, 969, 1004, 1036–1037, 1133–1135.

48. See six works by Henry George: *Progress and Poverty: An Inquiry into the Causes of Industrial Depressions and of Increase of Want with Increase of Wealth*, Fiftieth Anniversary Edition (New York: Robert Schalkenbach Foundation, 1942); *The Land Question: Property in Land the Condition of Labor* (New York: Robert Schalkenbach Foundation, 1965. Orig. pub. in 1881); *Protection of Free Trade: An Examination of the Tariff Question, with Especial Regard to the Interests of Labor* (New York: Robert Schalkenbach Foundation, 1966. Orig. pub. in 1886); *Social Problems* (New York: Robert Schalkenbach Foundation, 1966. Orig. pub. in 1883); *A Perplexed Philosopher: Being an Examination of Mr. Herbert Spencer's Various Utterances on the Land Question, With Some Incidental Reference to His Synthetic Philosophy* (New York: Robert Schalkenbach Foundation, 1965. Orig. pub. in 1892); *The Source of Political Economy* (New York: Robert Schalkenbach Foundation, 1968. Orig. pub. in 1897). For a discussion with much original material of George's views on the Chinese question, see Henry George, Jr., *The Life of Henry George* (New York: Robert Schalkenbach Foundation, 1960. Orig. pub. in 1900), pp. 191–203.

49. United States Senate, Forty-fourth Congress, *Report of the Joint Special Committee to Investigate Chinese Immigration*, p. 289.

50. Ibid., p. 282.

51. Ibid., p. 286.

52. Ibid.

53. Ibid., pp. 287–288.

54. *Ozawa vs. United States*, 260 U.S. 178 (1922); for particulars of this case see the Consulate-General of Japan, *Documental History of Law Cases Affecting Japanese in the United States, 1916–1924* (San Francisco: Consulate-General of Japan, 1925; reprint, New York: Arno Press, 1978), I, pp. 1–121.

55. Robert E. Park, "Racial Assimilation in Secondary Groups with Particular Reference to the Negro," in Robert E. Park, *Race and Culture: The Collected Papers of Robert E. Park*, vol. I, edited by Everett Cherrington Hughes et al. (Glencoe, IL: The Free Press, 1950), p. 209.

56. Henry George, "Why Work Is Scarce, Wages Low, and Labour Restless," address presented in the Metropolitan Temple in San Francisco, March 26, 1878. Quoted in Henry George, Jr., *The Life of Henry George*, p. 203.

57. Consulate-General of Japan, *Documental History of Law Cases*, II, pp. 1–1051; *Oyama vs. California*, 332 U.S. 633 (1947); and Audrie Girdner and Anne Loftis, *The Great Betrayal: The Evacuation of the Japanese Amer-*

icans During World War II (London: Collier-Macmillan, 1969), pp. 428–432.

58. George E. Pazzetta and Harry A. Kersey, Jr., "Yamato Colony: A Japanese Presence in South Florida," *Tequesta: The Journal of the Historical Association of Southern Florida*, XXXVI (1976), 66–77.

59. Jacobus ten Broek, Edward N. Barnhart, and Floyd W. Matson, *Prejudice, War and the Constitution* (Berkeley: University of California Press, 1954).

60. *Personal Justice Denied: Report of the Commission on Wartime Relocation and Internment of Civilians* (Washington, DC: U.S. Government Printing Office, December 1982); *Personal Justice Denied: Report of the Commission on Wartime Relocation and Internment of Civilians—Part 2: Recommendations* (Washington, DC: U.S. Government Printing Office, June 1983); Rockwell Chin et al., "The Long Road: Japanese Americans Move on Redress," *Bridge: Asian American Perspectives*, VII (Winter 1981–1982), 11–29; and Judith Miller, "Wartime Internment of Japanese Was 'Grave Injustice,' Panel Says," *New York Times*, February 25, 1983, pp. A1-A2.

61. Minoru Yasui, " 'Coram Nobis' to the Supreme Court," *Pacific Citizen*, April 16, 1982, pp. 2, 5; "3 Japanese-Americans Ask Court to Overturn Wartime Convictions," *New York Times*, January 31, 1983, p. A14; "Bad Landmark: Righting a Racial Wrong," *Time*, November 21, 1983, p. 51; David Margolick, "Legal Legend Urges Victims to Speak Out," *New York Times*, November 24, 1984, pp. 25, 26; Aaron Epstein, "Japanese Internment Cases to be Heard," *Miami Herald*, November 18, 1986, p. 15A; and two articles by Robert Shimabukuro, "Min Yasui Dies at 70; Services Held in Denver," and "Coram Nobis Attorney Says Yasui Appeal Will Continue," *Pacific Citizen*, November 21, 1986, pp. 1, 8. See also Gordon Hirabayashi, "Good Times, Bad Times: Idealism Is Realism," Sunderland P. Gardner Lecture, Canadian Yearly Meeting, August 14, 1985, Canadian Quaker Pamphlet No. 22 (Argenta, British Columbia, Canada: Argenta Friends Press, September 1985); and Peter Irons, *Justice at War: The Story of the Japanese American Internment Cases* (New York: Oxford University Press, 1983).

62. House of Representatives, Seventy-seventh Congress, 2d Session, *National Defense Migration. Hearings Before the Select Committee Investigating National Defense Migration* (Washington, DC: U.S. Government Printing Office, 1942; reprint, New York: Arno Press, 1978), pp. 11648–11650.

63. Ibid., pp. 10973–11023.

64. Fred H. Schmidt states:

The . . . minority groups mentioned here have lived in this region under social and economic conditions that are commonly associated with the fate of the Negro in the United States. The Indian, the Spanish Surnamed, the Oriental, the Negro—all of whom are of significant number in the region's population—can match among themselves their experiences with segregated housing, segregated schools, discriminating social treatment, repressed civil rights, and limited employment opportunites. . . . That so many . . . were seen as spicks, greasers, pepper bellies, niggers, japs, chinks, red skins, or as persons deserving some other contemptuous name . . . made it relatively easy to sort and segregate the non-Anglo. Those so sorted were not considered proper members of the dominant society.

Fred H. Schmidt, *Spanish Surnamed American Employment in the Southwest*, a study prepared for the Colorado Civil Rights Commission under the Auspices of the Equal Employment Opportunity Commission (Washington, DC: U.S. Government Printing Office, 1970), pp. 76–77.

65. Robert F. Heizer and Alan J. Almquist, *The Other Californians: Prejudice and Discrimination Under Spain, Mexico, and the United States to 1920* (Berkeley: University of California Press, 1971), pp. 96, 197. But see Paul S. Taylor, *Mexican Labor in the United States* (Berkeley: University of California Press, 1930; reprint, New York: Arno Press and *New York Times*, 1970), pp. 242–248.

66. Ringer, *"We the People" and Others*, pp. 968–969.

67. Ibid., p. 973.

68. *People vs. Hall*, 4 Cal. 399 (October 1, 1854). See Stanford M. Lyman, "Asian American Contacts Before Columbus: Alternative Understandings for Civilization, Acculturation, and Ethnic Minority Status in the United States," in Sohken Togami (ed.), *Japanese Americans: Iju Kara Jiritsu Eno Ayumi* (Kyoto, Japan: Mineruva Shobo, 1985), pp. 341–392.

69. *Cherokee Nation v. State of Georgia*, 5 Peters 1 (1831), at 34.

70. Ibid., at 16.

5

PUERTO RICANS: THE RAINBOW PEOPLE

Clara E. Rodriguez

The racial context that Puerto Ricans encountered when they entered the United States was at once contradictory and ironic. Puerto Ricans entered a heterogeneous society that articulated an assimilationist, melting-pot ideology but that, in fact, had evolved a racial order of dual ethnic queues, one white and one nonwhite.[1] It was a society that denied that difference should exist, while, at the same time, it tolerated and sometimes supported separate schools, jobs, and housing for those who were racially and/or ethnically "different." This race order was quickly and clearly perceived by Puerto Ricans. The irony was that Puerto Ricans represented the ideal of the American melting-pot ideology—a culturally unified, racially integrated people. However, this presented a problem to their acceptance in the United States. The dilemma that Puerto Ricans faced early on was essentially the need for them to regress to a more racist society (Robert Schwartz, professor of sociology, State University of New York–Stonybrook, personal correspondence, 1986).

RESEARCH LITERATURE ON RACE

Perceptual Dissonance

The imposition of the U.S. race order has meant the dominance of racial over cultural classification, that is, the division of Puerto Ricans and other Latinos into whites and nonwhites. Research in this area has found evidence of the strains this imposition has produced. The major findings in this area reflect the realization of the competing racial classification system (perceptual dissonance), the resistance of the U.S. system (intermediate classifications), and acceptance of compromise with the U.S. system (the "browning tendency," discussed later). The following discussion will review these findings and analyze the influence of important temporal and regional effects.

Findings from a 1972 study of fifty-two first- and second-generation Puerto Ricans in New York indicate that Puerto Ricans see themselves as racially different from the way they are seen by others (Rodriguez, 1974). Respondents were asked to classify themselves in terms of color; meanwhile, the interviewer also classified respondents in terms of color using U.S. racial classifications. These classifications were based on whether or not the person would be considered "white" by white Americans in a white setting; in other words, standing at a bus stop in Minneapolis, Minnesota, would the respondent be seen as white or nonwhite? Four U.S. categories resulted: white, black, and two intermediate categories—"possibly white" and "not white, not black." The latter two categories can be thought of as an intermediate "tan" group.

The major finding to emerge from this study was that a substantial proportion of respondents did not see themselves as the interviewer saw them. Objective perceptions—how they were seen—did not correspond with subjective perceptions—how they saw themselves. There was persistent perceptual dissonance with regard to racial classification.[2] Although some respondents classified themselves as lighter in skin color than they were perceived, a large number of respondents of both generations tended to classify themselves as darker than they were

Table 5.1
Racial Perceptions

	White	Tan	Black	Total
Self-perception				
Number	119	214	25	358
Percentage	33.24	59.78	6.98	100.00
North American Perception				
Number	202		145	347
Percentage	58.21	0.00	41.79	100.00

Source: Martinez (1988).

perceived by the interviewer. (This is referred to as the "browning tendency.")

A subsequent study by Angel R. Martinez (1988) of second-generation Puerto Rican college students in New York found similar results. The students were asked how they thought North Americans saw them and how they saw themselves. Table 5.1 illustrates the findings. When asked what color they were (white, black, or tan), the majority of the students (59.78 percent) said "tan," a third (33.24 percent) said "white," and a small minority (6.98 percent) said "black." When asked, however, how they felt North Americans saw them, 58.21 percent said "white" and 41.79 percent said "black." Clearly, many recognized a difference in how they saw themselves and how they were seen. Thus, the first study showed there was a difference, and the second showed that there was awareness of the difference on the part of Puerto Ricans sampled.[3]

Intermediate Classifications

What is perhaps most interesting in the results of these studies is the tendency of many respondents to place themselves in racially intermediate positions in the United States, that is, between black and white. Whether the term *tan* or Spanish-language terms such as *trigueño* are used, the point is that more respondents opted *not* to choose the clear white or black designation. This response parallels the 1980 Census results, which will be discussed later.

The Browning Tendency

Also of interest in the studies is the "browning tendency" (Rodriguez, 1974; Ginorio, 1979; Martinez, 1988). This is the name given to the phenomenon of some respondents seeing themselves as darker than they are seen by others. In the Martinez study, when respondents were asked how they thought North Americans perceived them, the percentage who said "black" increased from a racial self-perception of 7 percent to 42 percent. The percent who said "white" went from 33 percent (self-perception) to 58 percent (other perception). This indicates that many thought that North Americans see them as "black" even though only a small percentage see themselves this way. It also indicates that many who thought North Americans see them as "white" actually see themselves as tan or black (see Table 5.1). Thus, self-placement within the North American bifurcated system "browned" some respondents while it "blanched" others.

The "whitening" process is consistent with what has been normally assumed to underlie the racial-formation process among Latin Americans. Latin American racial terms and classification systems have tended to "lighten" individuals. This is implicit in what Peter Wade (1985: 243) has called the "*blanqueamiento*" (bleaching or whitening) tendency in Latin America and what Clara E. Rodriguez (1973, 1974) has referred to as "the preference for white" in Puerto Rico. (The studies do not explain why some respondents shifted from a darker self-perception to a lighter other perception within the North American racial classification system.) What is unexpected is the "browning tendency"; this contrasts strongly with the previous tradition of *blanqueamiento*. Why is the U.S. "melting pot" browning Puerto Ricans? Ada Elsa Izcoa (1985: 12b) found that Puerto Ricans in the United States appear to be adopting the North American conception of race for their own racial self-definition.

There are a number of factors that may be influencing this process. Regional setting can influence browning. The studies mentioned above took place in New York City, where juxtaposition of the term *black-and-Puerto Rican* with *white* is common and induces the conception of Puerto Ricans as a third nonwhite race (in recent years the more common term has become *blacks-and-Hispanics*). This conception of a third race has usually translated into something lighter than black and darker than white—that is, brown or tan.

Browning may also represent a political identification with "people of color."[4] Browning may reflect an ongoing struggle for racial redefinition. This struggle results from the clash of Puerto Ricans (perhaps of Latinos in general) with the U.S. race order. Although Puerto Ricans entered an essentially biracial society where integration was only one-way and where ethnicity or cultural differences were generally suppressed, the second generation came of age during the intense black power struggles. This younger group and subsequent Puerto Rican migrants encountered a society that was more intensely aware of its basic racial divisions and that was undergoing a racial transformation (Omi and Winant, 1983a, 1983b). This period of ferment crystallized the bipolar white/black distinctions in the system. In so doing, it may have forced the choice—to be white or black—for some Puerto Ricans, or it may have made them aware of the fact that the choice would be forced. In either case, the browning process reflects an accommodation to or compromise with the U.S. race order. In a broader sense, it reflects the ongoing struggle for racial definition.

Another ramification of this struggle (and perhaps another result of the black movement of the 1960s) may be seen in the large numbers who chose the intermediate racial classifications. The black movement, in reconceptualizing the meaning of *black*, also altered the meaning of *white* (Omi and Winant, 1983a: 35). The greatest triumph of the civil rights and black power movements was their ability to redefine racial identity and consequently race itself (Omi and Winant, 1983b: 35). They placed on the agenda the politics of difference.

The second generation of Puerto Ricans encountered a society that was undergoing a comprehensive reevaluation. These basic reevaluations and redefinitions undoubtedly had an impact on a group that was already (because of its unique political status, racial makeup, and economic position) at the crossroads of the basic issues contested: race, class, and gender. The intermediate racial classifications may have represented an alternate cultural-racial option to white and black.

RACIAL CLASSIFICATION AND THE CENSUS

That the United States has had difficulty coming to grips with the racial heterogeneity of Puerto Ricans and other Hispanics is reflected in the continuing debate over how to count Hispanics.[5] In 1930, Hispanics/Latinos were included in the Census as a racial category. In 1950 and 1960 they surfaced as "Persons of Spanish Surname and Spanish Mother Tongue." In 1970 they were "Persons of Both Spanish Surname and Spanish Mother Tongue" (Omi and Winant, 1983a: 56). By 1980, Hispanics had lobbied for the introduction of a new item on the 100 percent count of the decennial Census. This item asked specifically whether the person was Hispanic or of Spanish origin or descent and allowed individuals to specify whether they were Mexican, Puerto Rican, Cuban, or other Spanish/Hispanic. For the 1990 Census there was a proposal to abandon the 1980 format, and again there were new proposals on how to count Hispanics (see U.S. Bureau of the Census, 1984).

How Puerto Ricans and other Hispanics have been counted racially also illustrates the enigma that Latinos represent within the U.S. race context.[6] In the decennial Censuses of 1950, 1960, and 1970, Puerto Ricans were overwhelmingly classified as "white"—the proportion classified as black or Negro was always less than 10 percent. (In reality, it is likely that more than 10 percent of Puerto Ricans were viewed, and treated, as non-white.) In 1980 the special Hispanic identifier noted above was introduced. The 1980 Census also asked its usual race question, which asked "Is this person . . . " and provided check-off categories for white, black or Negro, Japanese, Chinese, Filipino, Korean, Vietnamese, American Indian, Asian Indian, Hawaiian, Guamanian, Samoan, Eskimo, Aleut, and other-specify.[7] The "other" category provided for a write-in response to race. (It is this last category that yielded the groups referred to subsequently as "other" and/or "Spanish.")

Thus, there were two questions asked: one to ascertain Span-

Table 5.2
Racial Self-Identification by Sex

	Male	Female	Total
White	5,459	6,920	12,379
	44.1	55.9	44.2
	45	43.6	
	19.5	24.7	
Black	513	582	1,095
	46.8	53.2	3.9
	4.2	3.7	
	1.8	2.1	
American Indian-Asian	20	17	37
	54.1	45.9	0.1
	0.2	0.1	
	0.1	0.1	
Spanish-write	5,597	7,718	13,315
	42.0	58.0	47.6
	46.1	48.6	
	20.0	27.6	
Other	540	633	1,173
	46.0	54.0	4.2
	4.5	4.0	
	1.9	2.3	
Column Total	12,129	15,870	27,999
	43.3	56.7	100

Chi-square	D.F.	significance	min E.F.	Cells w/
22.82328	4	0.0001	16.028	E.F.<5
				0

Source: 1980 Public Use Microdata Sample, 5% Sample, New York City Boroughs.

Note: For each category, first row indicates number, second row indicates column percentage, third row indicates raw percentage, and fourth row represents the cell's percentage of the total.

ish origin, and the other to ascertain race. An analysis of these two questions for Puerto Ricans in New York yielded some provocative results.[8] Less than 4 percent of Puerto Ricans in New York City identified themselves as black, only 44 percent as white, while the remainder (48 percent) responded they were "other" and wrote in a Spanish descriptor—Puerto Rican, Boricua, Hispanic, or the like (see Table 5.2).[9] These results seem to go against earlier social scientists' predictions.[10] It was thought that Puerto Ricans who were black would assimilate into the black community while those who were (or could pass for) white would assimilate into white, middle-class, suburban America and that a few would be left as ceremonial standard bearers of the Puerto Rican community (Mills, 1950: 133; Herberg, 1955:

56). It appears, on the face, that the few ceremonial standard bearers left—those who identified as "other, Spanish"—constitute the largest proportion of Puerto Ricans in New York City.

On the National Level

The tendency for all Hispanics to identify as "other" was also seen on the national level. Fully 40 percent of all Hispanics in the United States indicated their race as "other."[11] The percent of Hispanics classifying themselves as "black" on the national level was about the same (under 4 percent) in 1980 as in 1970, while the proportion of "white" Hispanics fell from 93.3 percent to 55.6 percent.[12] Thus, this is not just a Puerto Rican phenomenon. A substantial proportion of all Hispanics opted for the "other" category. Approximately 60 percent of the nation's Hispanic population is of Mexican origin. There are undoubtedly different racial identification patterns for different Spanish-origin groups.[13]

Hispanic Racial Classification by State

The distribution of Hispanic racial self-classification also varied by state. The proportion identifying as "other" varied from a low of 6 percent in West Virginia to a high of 48.5 percent in Kansas. Moreover, a multiple regression analysis of Hispanic racial identification by state indicated that the percentage of Hispanics identifying as "other" was positively related to the density of Hispanics in a state and negatively related to the proportion of blacks in a state.[14] (It was not related to the proportion of whites in a state.) Thus, the larger the number of Hispanics in the state, the greater the probability that Hispanics identified as "other"; the greater the number of blacks in the state, the lower the probability that Hispanics identified as "other."[15] Assuming there is no racial selectivity in migration to different states, the data indicate that Hispanic racial identification as "other" increases with relative Hispanic density and decreases with the proportion of blacks. It may be that the greater the proportion of blacks, that is, the more salient the biracial structure, the more likely Hispanics are to accept biracial classifications for themselves—as white or black. Conversely, the greater the number of Hispanics, the greater the tendency to identify as "other, Spanish."

However, these results focus only on one variable: proportional representation of Hispanics, whites, and blacks within states. It is possible that the different patterns of Hispanic racial identification within these states may be due to other demographic, economic, and/or political differences among states. Moreover, since they are state level data, they do not capture the finer details and influences of residence and socioeconomic status. Nonetheless, the data do point out two important facts: (1) the prevalent, but varying, pattern of Hispanic identification as "other"; and (2) the need to research this apparent variability. It may be that racial definitions and perceptions are structurally defined, just as class and gender are. In other words, race and racial self-perceptions may reflect the economic and political context within which social relations evolve.

Hispanic and U.S. Racial Classification Patterns

The pattern of Hispanic racial identification is drastically different from that of non-Hispanics in the United States. In 1980, the proportion of non-Hispanics identifying themselves as "other" was less than 2 percent in all the states, except Hawaii where it was 2.9 percent (U.S. Bureau of the Census, 1982). What does this mean? Why did 40 percent of the nation's Hispanics, and 48 percent of New York City's Puerto Ricans, answer they were "other" and explain they were "Spanish" (in some way) when asked to indicate their race? Some maintain they misunderstood the question. However, it seems unlikely that more than 7.5 million Hispanics would all misunderstand the question. Others might argue that these results indicate that these Hispanics considered themselves to be of another race. However, many Latinos would object to this interpretation.[16]

Latin American Race

On a social level, what is more probable is that Hispanics have a different conception of race, one that is as much cultural as it is racial. Jose Vazconcelos's (1966) early book *La Raza Cosmica* seems to suggest that in Mexico there was an amalgamation of cultures and peoples that produced a new stronger "race." Indeed, this concept has been a strong theme in Latin American literature and political thought (Munoz, 1982). The common use of the term *la raza* by and for Mexicans and Chicanos and the reference to Columbus Day in Puerto Rico as *El Dia de La Raza* (Race Day) seem to imply that there is a conception of "race" that differs from that prevalent in the United States. This conception may have had antecedents in Spain, may have been redefined in the colonial context, and may now be again in the process of redefinition in the United States.

Julian Pitt-Rivers (1975: 90) has argued that in Latin America the concept of race is equivalent to a concept of social race (see also Wagley, 1965). He says that although the concept of race in Latin America is unclear, as a minimal definition it "refers to a group of people who are felt to be somehow similar in their essential nature." He argues that the word "owes little to physical anthropology but refers . . . to the ways in which people are classified in daily life. What are called race relations are, in fact, always questions of social structure." This may shed light on why Hispanics answered they were "other" and wrote in a Spanish descriptor.

Mind-Sets Underlying Responses

On an individual level, we can logically derive a few reasons why Hispanics in the United States chose to be "other"; they saw themselves as racially "other"—as being tan, beige, or brown. Others may have been "other" by default—not white, not black, not either of these two colors, but another color or race. This is what the Census item intended to elicit, a racial response. But others may have responded culturally. They were Puerto Rican, Mexican, and so on. This did not necessarily imply a racial designation or classification. The presence on the Census form of separate categories for Koreans, Japanese, and other cultural categories of Asians may have increased the probability of a Hispanic cultural response (Tienda and Ortiz, 1984; Lowry, 1982).

Also possibly underlying the responses is a particular political mind-set. This is related to the cultural mind-set, but it represents a more conscious resistance to the black/white racial classification system of the United States. Here, there is a conscious choice to reject black/white racial classifications. In this case, the Spanish write-in classification represented not just a cultural response but a political one as well.

Finally, there is the mind-set of the person who answered the race item from the perspective of "this is how others see me." Although other people's perceptions should influence how one sees oneself, in racial situations, where opposing perceptions are always at work, this congruence may not always be present (see the earlier discussion on perceptual dissonance).

These different response modes and mind-sets are not necessarily mutually exclusive, although one may predominate most of the time. The mind-sets may also change with length of residence in the United States, perhaps with greater exposure to non-Hispanic settings, and with increasing levels of education. It is possible that the longer the time spent in the United States, the more individuals move away from the cultural response and toward the racial response, the cultural-political response, or the "as others see me" response. But which response mode predominated in the data, and why, we cannot say.

We can speculate but we cannot know definitively why Hispanics chose the "other" option to the extent that they did. What is evident, however, is that many Hispanics bypassed the "white" or "black" options, deciding they were neither of these. It seems very probable, then, that in declaring they were "other" and in writing in a Spanish descriptor, they were declaring a cultural-racial sense of identity that heretofore had not been noted in Census counts. It is possible that the 1980 Census captured (unwittingly) the tendency of Puerto Ricans (and other Hispanics) to identify themselves first culturally and then, perhaps, racially. This possibility requires further investigation. However, what the results indicate very clearly is that there is a substantial group of Hispanics who do not identify themselves in traditional U.S. racial terms.

RACE AND CLASS: AN ANALYSIS OF CENSUS DATA

Given the traditional relationships between race and class in the United States, the question that occurs is how these race groups are faring economically. For example, are "white" Puerto Ricans faring better economically than "black" Puerto Ricans? The larger question under which this is subsumed is whether the race order in the United States has impacted on the Puerto Rican community so as to produce different economic consequences for Puerto Ricans of different color. Do these race groups represent different social classes?[17] These questions were investigated using the 1980 Public Use Microdata Sample Census data. The results were intriguing.

Statistical analyses of this large sample indicate that racial classification is a significant stratifying variable within the New York City Puerto Rican community.[18] How Puerto Ricans classified themselves is significantly related to the socioeconomic position they occupied in New York City. However, the relationships found between race and economic status were somewhat unexpected.[19] Puerto Ricans identifying as "black" or "white" fared about the same, while those identifying as "other" (and writing in that they were Spanish) lagged far behind the first two groups.

For example, regardless of the income measure used (household income, family income, income from wages and salary, self-employment income, welfare, or income from all sources), the pattern was consistent: white Puerto Ricans were the most well-off, followed by black Puerto Ricans, while the "other, Spanish" group was in a distant third place. This is illustrated by the mean household incomes of the three groups, which were $14,444, $13,369, and $11,539 respectively. The race groups also differed significantly with regard to education, jobs, government employment, occupations, labor force participation, hours and weeks worked, and poverty levels, and the same pattern noted above generally held.[20] Thus, those who identified as "other,

Spanish" were, as a group, more disadvantaged than those who identified as white or black. They were less employed in the government sector, had fewer upper-level occupations, less college education, more unemployment, greater poverty, worked fewer hours and weeks, and were more concentrated in declining manufacturing areas.[21]

The Assimilation Hypothesis

It might be reasoned that the "other, Spanish" group was less successful because it was less assimilated, that perhaps its very classification as "other, Spanish" indicated a less assimilated stance.[22] Being less assimilated would put them at a greater disadvantage in the society. However, further analysis using such factors as birthplace, English proficiency, speaking Spanish at home, fertility rates, and age as measures of assimilation did not substantiate this hypothesis. The "other, Spanish" and the white groups appeared to be quite similar to each other, while both these groups were significantly different from the black group, which had higher proportions born in the United States and spoke "only English" at home.[23]

Puerto Ricans Born in the United States

Traditional theories of assimilation would lead to the expectation that Puerto Ricans born in the United States would tend to be more assimilated. Being more assimilated, they would therefore identify more as either white or black and choose the "other, Spanish" write-in classification less often. (This assumes, of course, that those born in the United States were also to a large degree raised there.) But the pattern of racial self-classification of those born in the states did not differ radically from that of Puerto Ricans born in Puerto Rico but living in New York.[24] The proportion identifying as "other, Spanish" was 48 percent in both cases. Being born in the United States seems to increase identification as black and to decrease identification as white. This provides some support for the browning tendency noted earlier.[25] It is of interest to note that: (1) the overwhelming majority (85 percent) of those born in the states still speak Spanish at home; and (2) the youth (ages 16 to 24) identify as "other, Spanish" to a greater degree than the population as a whole. (This may, to some extent, be affected by the fact that parents may have filled out the Census information for youth.)

Racial Identity Is in the Language

What may be more important than birthplace is where people have been socialized and for how long. Thus, one would expect to find that older, U.S.-born Puerto Ricans would identify less as "other, Spanish" and more as white or black. One would also expect the older group to speak less Spanish at home. This appears to be the case. Up to the age of 39, the majority of Puerto Ricans born in the states speak Spanish at home and identify as Spanish. Those 40 and over, on the other hand, increasingly identify as white or black. For Puerto Ricans born in Puerto Rico but living in New York City there is the same tendency to take on white and black racial classifications as age increases.[26]

The language used in the home also appears to play an important role in racial identification. Given that English-language-only groups—regardless of age—tended to identify more as white or black and less as "other, Spanish,"[27] speaking English at home seems to increase the likelihood that Puerto Ricans will identify as white or black, regardless of age. Thus, the hypothesis that Puerto Ricans born in the United States would be more assimilated and, hence, identify less as Spanish and more as either white or black held only for those who were older or for those who spoke only English at home. (Both these latter groups were relatively small in number.) This suggests that racial identity is to some extent carried or reflected in the language.

If these findings were to be used to predict the racial self-classification of those born in the United States, then the following could be said: If Puerto Ricans speak only English at home, they will tend to classify themselves as white or black, regardless of their age. If, on the other hand, they speak Spanish at home, then age is a factor, with those over 40 identifying more as white or black and those 39 or younger classifying themselves as Spanish as often or more often than the Puerto Rican group as a whole and as often or more often than those born in Puerto Rico but living in New York.

Gender, Race, and Class

Before proceeding to a discussion of the implications of these findings and of current trends, it is important to address the question of how gender has intersected with race and class for Puerto Ricans in the United States.[28] The distribution of Puerto Rican women's racial classification was similar to that of men.[29] In addition, among those born in the United States, there was the same tendency to identify as black. However, a significant theme in the data results was the significance of gender within race groups. That is, within the segmentation outlined above there was often a further division—that of gender. Thus, within each race group women often tended to be worse off than their respective men. They had higher rates of poverty and were less employed by the government or in higher-paying occupations. (However, more women were employed in the professional services area.) The differences between women tended to parallel those between men. Although the numbers were not large, there is some indication that Puerto Rican women who identified as black were exceptional in a number of ways: they were more represented in the professional services and went to college more than the men in their group; indeed their college attendance exceeded that of Puerto Rican men in all groups.

DISCUSSION AND IMPLICATIONS

Assimilation or Biculturation?

It may be that the assimilation measures used here (and generally elsewhere) are better measures of exposure and adaptation to the United States than of acceptance and assimilation. Thus, it may be that among the most "assimilated"—by these measures—there are also the most bicultural. That is to say, among those most assimilated (that is, those older individuals, most proficient in English, born in the United States, speaking the least Spanish at home, and with the fewest children) there may also be many who are interested in retaining their ethnic culture and identity. These individuals may have dual cultural identities; they are, in essence, bicultural. For these individuals, taking on the characteristics mentioned above does not necessarily mean accepting or endorsing the host country's norms and mores and rejecting those of their home country, as the term *assimilation* implies.

As Alejandro Portes and Robert L. Bach (1985) found in their study of Cuban immigrants, the acquisition of characteristics generally associated with assimilation in the United States need not mean that ethnic ties are weakened (see also Carillo et al., n.d.). Similarly, birthplace, by itself, is not indicative of greater assimilation for Puerto Ricans because of the strong migration and visiting flows back and forth between the states and the island. Moreover, the retention of cultural traits is not necessarily indicative of less assimilation and consequently less economic success. For example, the retention of the Spanish language at home has not been found (by itself) to have a negative impact on economic status (Tienda and Neidert, 1984). Alvin S. Rosenthal et al. (1983) found that speaking Spanish at home does not necessarily lead to lower attainment in math and reading among children in school; instead, they find there are differential effects.

The Future

It is apparent that age and language are factors in racial identification, but it is unclear what role these factors will play in the future of Puerto Ricans in the United States. It can be argued that as those born in the states age, they will settle into an acceptance of the race order, that is, of the race-over-culture racial classification system. If it is a question of settling (with age) into traditional U.S. racial classifications, then the future of the Puerto Rican community is fairly clearly laid out. As Giles Grenier (1984) argues, the language shift to English is completed by the age of 35, and this is indicative of Anglicization. After the age of 35, little language shift is to be expected because people have settled into the labor market, gotten married, and been more exposed to the language spoken outside of the early childhood family. In this case, as the large population of Puerto Ricans who migrated in the 1950s and 1960s ages, the community will become increasingly self-perceived as black and white.

However, it can also be argued that when these data were collected these over-40 Puerto Ricans, who were born in the states and who identified more strongly as white or black, were less involved in the upheaval of the 1960s when cultural and racial identification became more closely linked (Mohr, 1987). If identity was a question of socialization during the 1960s, then the future is less clear, for we do not know what impact this experience has had and will continue to have on the current and future generations of Puerto Ricans. The settling and the 1960s socialization hypotheses are not mutually exclusive. However, they both require further sensitive investigation with more qualitative data.[30]

Emerging Trends

Race is a social category.[31] In the same way that gender has come to be separated from biological sex, so too biological race can be distinguished from social definitions of race. Since race is to a large extent socially constructed, racial definitions can change from society to society. This is evident in Charles Wagley's (1965) example of the man who, traveling from Puerto Rico to Mexico to the United States, changes his race from white to Mulatto to Negro. It is also evident in South Africa's designation of the Japanese as "honorary" whites in their country, in Nazi Germany's designation of Jews as a race, and in the reference to East Indians, Pakistanis, and South Americans as blacks in Great Britain. (In the United States, where race has been more biologically defined, the social or cultural dimensions of race have been less evident—although they have, nonetheless, existed.) Race as a social category also changes over time. Five trends are evident now in the Puerto Rican community as the clash between biological and social concepts of race continues: the use of white and black as cultural terms, the concept of being nonwhite by default, the use of contextual racial definitions, the use of deflected racial classification, and the emergence of racial "chameleons."

White and Black as Cultural Terms. Some of the trends emerging in the intense, but quiet, struggle over racial definition, that is, the race vs. cultural criterion, have yet to show up in literature or to be measured.[32] One such trend is the increasingly common use, by Puerto Ricans (and by other Hispanics), of the term *white* as a cultural designator. Earlier groups of Puerto Ricans referred to white Americans as *americanos* and black Americans as *morenos* or *negros*; cultural subdivisions were also used when appropriate—*italianos, judios, haitianos,* and so on. In effect, and quite consistent with tradition, groups were perceived culturally—not as white or nonwhite.

Today the term *white* is commonly used as a cultural and not as a racial term. This is especially common among second- and third-generation Puerto Ricans as well as many other second-generation Latinos in urban areas. Thus, in speaking of speech, dress norms, attitudes, and other important criteria of status or friendship definition, Puerto Ricans and other Latinos will say quite often "He or she is white," or "But that's so white." Whites have become a cultural group. In the same way that ethnics are (culturally) identified by Americans (as non-Hispanics) as "the Puerto Rican boy" or "the Spanish woman," so now Americans are referred to as "the white guy," "the white woman," or, for purposes of identification, "You know, the white one." Such classifications immediately distinguish the person within a group of "similarly white-looking" Hispanics or first-generation Italians.

This cultural use of the word *white* is used by Latinos of all colorations and racial self-perceptions. The significance and depth of this change was evident when recently a Puerto Rican college professor described, in passing, a black-looking Hispanic as "culturally black." Thus, to be black is not just to be a member of a race, for Latinos can be racially black but culturally Spanish. It is to be a member or representative of a culture. Similarly, Latinos can be seen to be racially white, but not be culturally white. Indeed, some have used the term *Spanish-White* as opposed to *white-white.*

This dimension is not so new, but it is more acknowledged

or more acceptable today than it was in the past. What is new today is the prevalence with which the term *white* is used and how culturally specific it is, as it is used for assimilated white Americans. In the past, the term *American* would have been used in its stead. In essence, what appears to be happening is that Puerto Ricans (and perhaps other Latinos) are using U.S. racial terms as cultural terms. However, the racial terms have apparently not totally lost their original significance or their connotations of dominance or power.[33] *White*, as a cultural term, is only used indirectly to refer to a person or a group—it is generally not openly used in the company of whites, for there is the expectation that they would be offended.

It appears there has been both some change and some continuity with regard to racial definitions. Originally, Puerto Ricans perceived, within each of the two categories—white and non-white—spectrums of color, of facial features, of hair texture, of bodily form, and of cultural predisposition that determined what kind of nonwhite or, for that matter, what kind of white one was. Thus, Puerto Ricans perceived different groups of people in a basically cultural way that, nonetheless, also took account of racial difference. Increasingly today, Puerto Ricans appear to be perceiving racial categories culturally. Culture continues to be foremost, but change is evident in the fact that North American race has become culture. This change is a result of the clash between the racial order in the United States and Puerto Rican/Latino racial attitudes and perceptions.

Nonwhite by Default. Another curious result of the interaction of Puerto Ricans with the race order in the United States is the default designation of Puerto Ricans and Latinos and nonwhite. (This has occurred somewhat in tandem with the use of *white* as a cultural term.) To the unreflecting Americanized mind, if Latinos are not white, they must be nonwhite.

At the research level, excruciating mental steps are taken to be precise about racial designations and yet not offend anyone. The result is often a fairly cumbersome, almost unintelligible system of categorization. For example, academics have often used the following racially precise but convoluted categories: nonwhite, non-Hispanic, non-Hispanic white, and any combination thereof. These are attempts to come to terms with the fact that two categories are based on race and one on culture. The new labels may be correct, but they are somewhat removed from the reality of life for each group, which is that they usually live as whites, blacks, or Hispanics.

The search for multiple categories, however, reflects the difficult dilemma of imposing the U.S. racial order on Puerto Ricans and other Latinos. It may be that the perpetuation of racism demands an either/or logic, otherwise the system would crumble. If classified racially, Latinos would subdivide into a continuum of racial categories. If they are not all white, they are nonwhite. Thus, in the popular lexicon Latinos are often classified as nonwhite by default.

Contextual Racial Definition. To a certain extent, race is always contextually defined. Exemplifying this point is the classic story of the survey researcher who is unaware that he is interviewing two-thirds of an interracial family, the white father and his white-appearing son. When the black mother returns from shopping, the researcher erases quietly, but quickly, his previous racial classification of the child, changing it from white to black. The child's race is changed because the context within which the child is viewed changes.

For Puerto Ricans and other Latinos there are similar contextual cues that define their "Hispanicity."[34] Those who can control the contextual cues to their ethnicity often do so. Some of the most common contextual cues are surname, accent, residence, friendship networks, religion, schools attended, music preferences, and sometimes political views (for example, sympathy for civil rights, bilingual education, and minority issues). The manipulation of these cues or symbols becomes for many the way in which they cope with the varying receptions they are given as a result of their being Hispanic. Many Hispanics unconsciously control contextual cues as a way of "testing the waters" before revealing they are Hispanic. Thus, in business, particularly in sales, last names are not initially mentioned, while in social situations or at times when the seller and buyer are both Latino, last names are stressed. This manipulation of contextual cues is not novel. All immigrants to the United States have participated in this game. What makes the Latino situation different is that this manipulation of cues can lead to more than one racial classification, and the definition of a person as Latino connotes, for some, a subtle (although often undefined and ambiguous) racial difference.[35]

Deflected Race. In a society as racially diverse as Puerto Rico, and with the legacies of slavery, colonialism, and the Spanish Inquisition, there has probably always been a concern with being classified as nonwhite or less white. It is very likely that the presence of darker members in the family has always been downplayed, that they have been relegated to the background, while those who were lighter or more European-looking have been advanced as the family's representative claim to the white race. In Puerto Rico, where racial classification often follows appearance, this has been possible. But in the United States, where racial classification follows ancestry, this has been more difficult to control. Consequently, in the United States Latino families are more determinant of individual classification. If a member of the family is deviant from the European white physical type, this is enough to send the whole family to another race. Given the diversity of Latino families in the United States and their large size (which increases the probability of diversity within families), many Latinos in the United States experience deflected racial classification.

The use of children to determine the racial identity of parents is an example of deflected race, as is the use of sibling(s) to determine another sibling's race. Deflected race categorization can also be seen as an extension of contextual definitions of race. It is the opposite of the Census example given above where the child of a mixed marriage was automatically classified as black regardless of his phenotypic appearance. In the case of deflected race categorization, if Latino children appear to be slightly "colored," then their parents (regardless of their phenotypic appearance) are also designated as black or "colored." This does not happen to white parents who are presumed to have adopted the children or to have participated in an interracial union. With the Latino family, it is not assumed that the child is adopted but rather that the family is not white. Deflected race classification is increasingly a part of Latino living in the United States.

Chameleons. "Perceptual dissonance" sounds like the name of a disease. The reality, while neither infectious nor disabling, is no less painful for being merely a state of mind. The experience of being seen in a way different from the way one sees oneself, particularly as it pertains to race, is clearly an unsettling process. Indeed, it has often been maintained that for the migrating Puerto Rican, the experience of racial reclassification, and its attendant racism, "frequently undermines the sense of autonomy and initiative . . . and leaves a residue of self-doubt and inadequacy" (Longres, 1974: 67). John F. Longres (1974) argues that this initial shock and its result persist as a psychological dilemma even among the seemingly assimilated.

However, there is also another, perhaps more positive but unresearched, side to perceptual dissonance: the chameleon-like quality that many second-generation Puerto Ricans have developed to adjust to the separate white, black, and Hispanic worlds within which they travel.[36] This may be rooted in the ability to see oneself in a variety of ways. Not everyone is capable of making these transitions completely, but many Puerto Ricans exhibit more flexibility and adaptability in these shifts than others who are more monocultural. Puerto Ricans become bi- and tricultural in addition to having language versatility.[37] These abilities to adapt and be flexible are generally not assessed in standardized tests of achievement or intelligence. Nor are they usually discussed in literature. Nonetheless, such individuals' abilities and talents are important and should be recognized by the educational system and the wider society.

CONCLUSION

The preceding material raises many important questions. What is the significance of the trends cited? What role does the economic structure have in influencing racial self-classification? Are those who identify themselves as white or black more successful because they identify as white or as black? Are they more successful because they are identified by others as white or as black? Does success lead them to identify themselves as white or as black? Why do so few identify as black? We cannot yet provide definitive conclusions. What cannot be denied, however, is that we are witnessing the strongest challenge ever to the U.S. bifurcation of race.[38]

NOTES

1. The term *dual queues* refers to the hierarchical ordering of ethnic-racial groups that has historically characterized the United States. These dual job and mobility queues are the result of successive waves of immigrants into a white/nonwhite racial order (see Rodriguez, 1973).

2. Melvin Tumin and Arnold Feldman (1961: 228) also note that in Puerto Rico, there was a difference between how Puerto Ricans were classified by Puerto Rican interviewers and how they classified themselves.

3. It should be noted that although the studies cited here had substantial numbers of respondents, they were purposive, judgment, or exploratory samples, not probability samples. Thus, generalizability to all Puerto Ricans or Hispanics in New York is limited.

4. For example, in the Rodriguez (1974) study there were a number of respondents who would have been perceived as white by North Americans but who nonetheless responded that they were brown because they identified with the political movements of American blacks and/or the oppressed in the Third World.

5. A considerable amount of organized community activity and struggle has always accompanied Census changes. See Michael Omi and Howard Winant (1983b), Marta Tienda and Vilma Ortiz (1984).

6. The enigmatic situation that Puerto Ricans present was evident in the debates over the 1970 Census count of Puerto Ricans. Puerto Rican groups demanded that third-generation Puerto Ricans be included in the count, pointing out that Blacks are counted as blacks regardless of generation. The U.S. Bureau of the Census considered Puerto Ricans as it had previous European immigrant groups. However, as one community leader stated: "We are considered Puerto Ricans no matter how long we are here" (Kihss, 1972: 15).

7. The Census used the same question in 1970 that it used in 1980; the only difference was that in 1980 it added the following to the listing of groups: Vietnamese, Asian Indians, Guamanians, Samoans, Eskimos, and Aleuts (Lowry, 1982).

8. The 5 percent Public Use Microdata Sample from the 1980 Census was the basis of this analysis. Only those over 16 years old were included in the sample, which initially consisted of 27,999 Puerto Ricans residing in the five New York City boroughs. With the exclusion of Puerto Ricans who classified themselves Asian, American Indian, and other-unspecified, 26,806 remained in the sample. (Puerto Ricans responding that they were Asian or American Indian were omitted because of the small sizes of these categories. The other-unspecified group

was also eliminated from the analysis because preliminary runs indicated the group did not follow a consistent pattern.) Chi square and analysis of variance were used to determine whether racial classification was a significant stratifying variable within the New York City Puerto Rican community. For additional research in this area, see Rodriguez (1989).

9. Another 4 percent responded they were "other" but did not write in a Spanish descriptor; about 1 percent responded they were Asian or Native American Indian (1980 Public Use Microdata Statistics [PUMS]).

10. These are the results of the 1980 Census. It is unknown if this represents a significant departure from previous Censuses. In the past, Puerto Ricans who might have checked off "other" and written in that they were Puerto Rican, Spanish, or another Hispanic descriptor were counted as white. Direct comparisons with Puerto Ricans in Puerto Rico are also impossible because the decennial Census form of 1980 did not collect or publish data on the racial classification of Puerto Ricans.

11. About 95 percent of all the 1980 Census questionnaires were self-administered; therefore the data reflects self-classification.

12. In 1970, of the 9.1 million Hispanics in the United States, 87,930 Spanish-origin persons classified themselves as "other," making for less than 1 percent in that category. Data on racial classification in 1970 were derived from the 1970 Census of Population, Subject Report Series, Persons of Spanish Origin, PC(2)–1C, Table 2.

13. Francois Nielson and Robert M. Fernandez (1981: 12) provide some evidence of different racial identification patterns for different Spanish-origin groups. Their study of high school students found that 59 percent of Puerto Rican high school seniors in the United States said they were "other," compared with 52 percent of Mexican, 9 percent of Cuban, and 21 percent of other Latin American seniors.

14. For analyses of the role of Hispanic density in economic outcomes, see Marta Tienda and Ding-Tzann Lii (1987) and Frank Bonilla (1985: 161).

15. The relationship between the proportion of the state population that is white and the proportion of Hispanics identifying as "other" was not statistically significant. Beta coefficients for the other two variables were statistically significant at the .001 level of significance, $F(3.47) = 6.995$. The equation used was as follows: $y(i) = B + m1x1(i) + m2x2(i) + m3x3(i)$, where $y(i)$ = Hispanics identifying as "other" as a proportion of total Hispanics within each state; $x1$ = white population as a proportion of total population within each state; $x2$ = black population as a proportion of total population within each state; $x3$ = a dummy variable for Hispanic density, coded 1 for states where His-

panic population exceeded 100,000. (Reimers, 1984, and Tienda, 1983: 257, both find a strong relationship between the concentration of Hispanics and lower income for Hispanics.)

More detailed information on the regression analysis is available from the author upon request. Data derived from the 1980 Census of Population, Persons of Spanish Origin by State: 1980, Supplementary Report, PC80-S1-7, Tables 4 and 5. Issued August 1982.

16. This interpretation was, in some ways, tested. In light of the Hispanic responses to race, the Census recently proposed to count Hispanics as a race. The proposal was so strongly opposed "through the most aggressive campaign ever seen by the bureau" that agency officials decided to abandon the proposal, fearing it would cause a withdrawal of needed community support (quote from McKenney, director of the U.S. Bureau of the Census, cited in *Hispanic Link Weekly Report*, May 26, 1986). It was clear from the Hispanic opposition encountered that Hispanics did not perceive themselves to be a race. This stands to reason, for Puerto Ricans and other Hispanics are not races, they are cultures. There are distinct ways of viewing races as well as different mixes of races within these cultures.

17. An earlier study using 1950 data tested a similar question—how race and culture influenced economic outcomes. Although results between black and white Puerto Ricans were inconclusive, Katzman (1978) found black Puerto Ricans to be "more successful in obtaining white collar jobs," but less remunerated for their jobs and also more subject to unemployment than black Anglos.

18. See note 6 for a description of the sample.

19. Assuming that the greater the self-perceived coloration of Puerto Ricans, the greater the socioeconomic disadvantage, it was hypothesized that Puerto Ricans who identified themselves as "white" would do best on standard socioeconomic indicators, those who identified as "other, Spanish" would do second best, and those who identified as "black" would do worst. Differences between groups were statistically significant with regard to all of the economic variables at the.05 level and below.

20. There was some indication that the group identifying itself as black was rather heterogeneous in composition. Despite high mean incomes and an advantaged position on a variety of variables, this group also registered higher proportions of individuals suffering long-term unemployment and looking for work. Thus, the picture that emerged was one where the white and black groups fared better (economically and educationally) than the "other, Spanish" group but where the relatively higher means and proportions of the black group may have been skewed by a small subgroup of advantaged individuals.

21. There were only slight deviations from this pattern. One was the income derived from self-employment: the "other, Spanish" group derives slightly more income from self-employment than blacks. Another was that Spanish males participate in the labor force, work as many weeks and hours, and are "looking for a job" as much as black males. Finally, black men and women suffered most from long-term unemployment.

22. In many respects, to give a cultural response to a racial question is to speak from the primacy of a cultural framework while to choose classification as "white" or "black" implies that racial contest is primary. (Although classification as "white" or "black" need not necessarily imply endorsement of the racial system, to a degree it implies acceptance of the racial terms.)

23. It is possible that, even though just as many in the "other, Spanish" group were born in the states as the white group, they spent less total time in the United States. If this were the case, they may have been less exposed to assimilating forces. (The fact that the Spanish group is younger may be indicative of less time in the United States.) However, since the Census does not contain date-of-entry information for Puerto Ricans, this question could not be addressed directly.

24. The pattern for women born in the United States deviated slightly from the general pattern of racial classification for all Puerto Ricans. A slightly higher proportion of women born in the United States identified as white and as black while a lower proportion identified as "other, Spanish." The differences, however, were very small. Men born in the states identified more as black and less as white while the "other, Spanish" classification remained virtually the same.

25. Generalizations here are hazardous, however, because of the relatively small numbers in the black cells.

26. However, the group born in Puerto Rico identifies more strongly as Spanish in the younger age groups and less strongly as white or black in the older age group.

27. There is still a significant subgroup that identifies as "other, Spanish," but it is less than 25 percent in all age groups.

28. The question of which of these variables (race, class, or gender) has the greatest weight in women's lives has been the subject of much debate. See, for example, Bel Hooks (1981, 1984), Gloria Joseph (1981), Angela Jorge (1983), Maxine Baca Zinn (1979), June Nash and Maria Patricia Fernandez-Kelly (1983), Elizabeth Higgenbotham (1985), Clara E. Rodriguez (1981, 1984), and Angela Ginorio (1979).

29. As Table 5.2 shows, there were some interesting, but not major differences by gender—for instance, more women saw themselves as

"other" and more men saw themselves as "white" or "black." But an analysis of variance on a small sample of 1,395 indicated these gender differences were not statistically significant.

30. The Census is the only source with a sufficiently large number of observations to allow a broad overview of the Latino race phenomena. Although the Census data yield an analysis of considerable breadth, by their very nature they lack the necessary depth. These data also raise questions that can be answered only through qualitative analysis involving in-depth interviews with a large number of individuals in their family and social contexts. Preferably, these would be part of a series of longitudinal studies. Only in this way would it be possible to capture the complex and subtle dynamics as people move from one society to another. These dynamics are extraordinarily difficult to measure, both on individual and aggregate levels. Such a study can constitute the subject of its own book. It would reveal a wealth of critical information about America's race consciousness and racial formation that, at present, does not exist.

31. Edgar T. Thompson (1975), Oliver C. Cox (1948), and Charles Hirschman (1986) employ this perspective in their work, but Jorge Duany (1985) provides the most relevant discussion of how the economic structures that developed in Puerto Rico and Cuba have influenced the particular racial attitudes, perceptions, and relations in each country.

32. I am indebted to comments from my students and family for heightening my own awareness of these trends.

33. The same question can be raised with regard to the racial terms in Puerto Rico: To what extent have they lost their original connotations of power or lack of power?

34. For an excellent discussion of the determinants of "Hispanicity" among Puerto Ricans and Mexicans in Chicago, see Felix Padilla (1985).

35. The results of a class survey by Jose Hernandez at Hunter College, City University of New York (CUNY), are intriguing in this regard. Students in a Puerto Rican community class were asked whether or not *Latino* was a purely ethnic term (the way people act) or a racial term (the way people look). The great majority (83 percent) said racial and ethnic, while only 14 percent said ethnic; only one person said neither. This indicates that the term *Latino* may be taking on racial connotations in the United States that it did not have in Latin America.

36. A similar concept is discussed briefly by Diane de Anda (1984) who describes the cognitive styles of bicultural individuals and the degree to which their styles mesh with the majority culture. Implicit in the meshing is a repertoire of styles and switching ability for bicultural individuals.

John Attinasi (1985) also finds the same switching ability in his study of East Harlem residents. He finds that residents switch from black English to various types of Spanish to various levels of English. This, he argues, represents a diverse array of linguistic and communicative skills, which suggest a variety of writing and reading abilities (see also Torruellas, 1986).

37. The question can be raised whether this chameleon-like quality will prevent Puerto Ricans from assimilating—that is, whether they are adopting bicultural skills without assimilating in the usual sense.

38. It might be argued that for multiracial groups, such as Puerto Ricans, there is bound to be a redefinition in the "fatherland" of not just ethnicity but also of individual racial identity (Blauner, 1972; Nelson and Tienda, 1985; Yetman and Steele, 1975). We would expect ethnicity and race to be redefined according to social psychological experiences, as well as placement in the labor market.

REFERENCES

Attinasi, John. 1985. "Language Attitudes and Working Class Ideology in a Puerto Rican Barrio of New York." *Ethnic Groups* 5: 55–78.

Baca Zinn, Maxine. 1979. "The Costs of Exclusionary Practices in Women's Studies." *Journal of Women in Culture and Society* 11 (21): 290–303.

Blauner, Robert. 1972. *Racial Oppression in America*. New York: Harper & Row.

Bonilla, Frank. 1985. "Ethnic Orbits: The Circulation of Peoples and Capital." *Contemporary Marxism* 10: 148–167.

Carrillo, Emilio, Richard Levins, Joseph Regna, Ellen Rak, Maria Gordian, and Ruberto Diaz. n.d. "Eco-Social Analysis: Evaluating the Health Relevant Social Environment of Migrant Latinos." Unpublished.

Cox, Oliver C. 1948. *Caste, Class and Race*. Garden City, NY: Doubleday.

de Anda, Diane. 1984. "Bicultural Socialization: Factors Affecting the Minority Experience." *Social Work* (March–April): 101–107.

Duany, Jorge. 1985. "Ethnicity in the Spanish Caribbean: Notes on the Consolidation of Creole Identity in Cuba and Puerto Rico, 1762–1868." *Ethnic Groups* 6: 99–123.

Ginorio, Angela. 1979. "A Comparison of Puerto Ricans in New York with Native Puerto Ricans and Native Americans on Two Measures of Acculturation: Gender Role and Racial Identification." Ph.D. dissertation, Fordham University, New York.

Grenier, Giles. 1984. "Shifts to English as Usual by Americans of Spanish Mother Tongue." *Social Science Quarterly* 65: 537–550.

Herberg, Will. 1955. *Protestant, Catholic, Jew*. Garden City, NY: Doubleday.

Higgenbotham, Elizabeth. 1985. "Race and Class Barriers to Black Women's College Attendance." *Journal of Ethnic Studies* 13 (1): 89–108.

Hirschman, Charles. 1986. "The Making of Race in Colonial Malaya." *Sociological Forum* 1 (2): 330–361.

Hooks, Bel. 1981. *Ain't I a Woman: Black Women and Feminism*. Boston: South End.

———. 1984. *Feminist Theory from Margin to Center*. Boston: South End.

Izcoa, Ada Elsa. 1985. "A Comparative Study of the Self-Images of Puerto Rican Adolescents: Immigrants and Non-Migrants," in Hilda Hidalgo and Joan L. McEniry (eds.), *Hispanic Temas*. Newark, N.J.: Rutgers University, Puerto Rican Studies Program.

Jorge, Angela. 1983. "Issues of Race and Class in Women's Studies: A Puerto Rican Woman's Thoughts, 1981," in Amy Swerdlow and Hanna Lessinger (eds.), *Class, Race and Sex: The Dynamics of Control*. Boston: G. K. Hall.

Joseph, Gloria. 1981. "The Incompatible Menage à Trois: Marxism, Feminism, and Racism," in Lydia Sargent (ed.), *Women and Revolution*. Boston: South End.

Katzman, Martin. 1978. "Discrimination, Subculture and the Economic Performance of Negroes, Puerto Ricans and Mexican-Americans." *American Journal of Economics and Society* 27 (4): 371–375.

Kihss, Peter. 1972. "A Latin Dispersal in City Reported." *New York Times*, July 2, p. 15.

Longres, John F. 1974. "Racism and Its Effects on Puerto Rican Continentals." *Social Casework* (February): 67–99.

Lowry, Ira S. 1982. "The Science and Politics of Ethnic Enumeration," in Winston A. Van Horne (ed.), *Ethnicity and Public Policy*, vol. 1. Madison: University of Wisconsin Press.

Martinez, Angel R. 1988. "The Effects of Acculturation and Racial Identity on Self-Esteem and Psychological Well-Being Among Young Puerto Ricans." Ph.D. dissertation, City University of New York.

Mills, C. Wright, Clarence Senior, and Rose Goldsen. 1950. *The Puerto Rican Journey: New York's Newest Migrants*. New York: Harper & Bros.

Mohr, Robert. 1987. "Puerto Ricans in New York: Cultural Evolution and Identity," in Asela Rodriguez de Laguna (ed.), *Images and Identities: The Puerto Rican in Two World Contexts*. New Brunswick, NJ: Transaction.

Munoz, Braulio. 1982. *Sons of the Wind: The Search for Identity in Spanish American Indian Literature*. New Brunswick, NJ: Rutgers University Press.

Nash, June, and Maria Patricia Fernandez-Kelly (eds.). 1983. *Women, Men, and the International Division of Labor*. New York: SUNY-Albany.

Nelson, Candace, and Marta Tienda. 1985. "The Structuring of Hispanic Ethnicity: Historical and Contemporary Perspectives." *Ethnic and Racial Studies* 8 (January): 49–74.

Nielson, Francois, and Roberto M. Fernandez. 1981. *Hispanic Students in American High School: Background Characteristics and Achievement*. Washington, DC: National Opinion Research Center, National Center for Education Statistics.

Omi, Michael, and Howard Winant. 1983a. "By the Rivers of Babylon: Race in the United States (Part One: Resurgent Racial Conflict in the 1980s)." *Socialist Review* 71 (September-October): 31–66.

————. 1983b. "By the Rivers of Babylon: Race in the United States (Part Two: The Great Transformation)." *Socialist Review* 72 (November-December): 35–68.

Padilla, Felix. 1985. *Latino Ethnic Consciousness: The Case of Mexican-Americans and Puerto Ricans in Chicago*. Notre Dame, IN: University of Notre Dame Press.

Pitt-Rivers, Julian. 1975. "Race, Color, and Class in Central America and the Andes," in Norman R. Yetman and C. Hoy Steele (eds.), *Majority and Minority*. Boston: Allyn & Bacon.

Portes, Alejandro, and Robert L. Bach. 1985. *Latin Journey: Cuban and Mexican Immigrants in the United States*. Berkeley: University of California Press.

Reimers, Cordelia. 1984. "The Wage Structure of Hispanic Men: Implications for Policy." *Social Science Quarterly* 65 (June).

Rodriguez, Clara E. 1969. "Political Legitimacy." Master's thesis, Cornell University.

————. 1973. "The Ethnic Queue: The Case of Puerto Ricans." Doctoral dissertation, Washington University, St. Louis, MO.

————. 1974. "Puerto Ricans: Between Black and White." *New York Affairs* 1 (4): 92–101.

————. 1981. "Triple Jeopardy and an Ethnic Studies Department," in George Mims (ed.), *The Minority Administrator in Higher Education: Progress, Experiences, and Perspectives*. New York: Schenkman.

————. 1984. "Hispanics and Hispanic Women in New York State." Paper prepared for the First Legislative Research Conference, Albany, January 21.

———. 1989. "Race, Class, and Gender among Puerto Ricans in New York." Report submitted to the Inter-University Program for Latino Research/Social Science Research Council, University of Texas, Austin, January.

Rosenthal, Alvin S., Kevin Baker, and Alan Ginsburg. 1983. "The Effect of Language Background on Achievement Level and Learning Among Elementary School Students." *Sociology of Education* 56 (October): 157–169.

Thompson, Edgar T. 1975. "The Plantation as a Race Making Situation in Plantation Societies, Race Relations and the South: The Regimentation of Populations," in *Selected Papers of Edgar T. Thompson*. Durham, NC: University Press.

Tienda, Marta. 1983. "Nationality and Income Attainment among Native and Immigrant Hispanic Men in the United States." *Sociological Quarterly* 24 (Spring): 253–272.

Tienda, Marta, and Ding-Tzann Lii. 1987. "Migration, Market Insertion and Earnings Determination of Mexicans, Puerto Ricans, and Cubans." University of Wisconsin, Institute for Research on Poverty, DP #830–87.

Tienda, Marta, and Lisa J. Neidert. 1984. "Language, Education and the Socioeconomic Achievement of Hispanic Origin Men." *Social Science Quarterly* 65 (June): 519–536.

Tienda, Marta, and Vilma Ortiz. 1984. " 'Hispanicity' and the 1980 Census." Center for Demography and Ecology (CDE), University of Wisconsin, Madison, CDE Working Paper 84–23.

Torruellas, Rosa. 1986. "The Failure of the New York Public Educational System to Retain Hispanic and Other Minority Students" (statement submitted to the New York State Black and Puerto Rican Labor Legislative Caucus, March 24, 1986). *Centro de Estudios Puertorriquenos Newsletter* (June).

Tumin, Melvin, and Arnold Feldman. 1961. *Social Class and Social Change in Puerto Rico*. Princeton, NJ: Princeton University Press.

U.S. Bureau of the Census. 1982. *Persons of Spanish Origin by State: 1980* (Supplementary Report PC80-S1-7, August). Washington, DC: U.S. Government Printing Office.

———. 1984. *Development of Race and Spanish Origin Questions for the 1990 Census* (background statement, Office of the Director, December). Washington, DC: Government Printing Office.

Vazconcelos, Jose. 1966. *La Raza Cosmica*, 3rd ed. Mexico City: Espasa-Calpe.

Wade, Peter. 1985. "Race and Class: The Case of South American Blacks." *Ethnic and Racial Studies* 8 (April): 233–249.

Wagley, Charles. 1965. "On the Concept of Social Race in the Americas," in Dwight B. Health and Richard N. Adams (eds.), *Contemporary Cultures and Societies of Latin America: A Reader in the Social Anthropology of Middle and South America and the Caribbean.* New York: Random House (originally published in 1959).

Yetman, Norman R., and C. Hoy Steele (eds.). 1975. *Majority and Minority.* Boston: Allyn & Bacon.

6

IRANIANS IN AMERICA: CONTINUITY AND CHANGE

Maboud Ansari

Never before in Iran's history have so many families and particularly young people fled that country. By Western count, over 2 million Iranians have left Iran since the 1978 revolution. The 1986 Iranian population of the United States was estimated to be between 245,000 to 341,000. Large numbers of expatriate Iranians also reside in Canada, Britain, France, Germany, Sweden, Denmark, Spain, Italy, Greece, Pakistan, Turkey, and Israel.

Iranian immigrants are relatively unique among ethnic groups who have emigrated to the United States. In fact, Iranian emigration is not only one of scientists, professionals, entrepreneurs, other talents, and cultural traditions but also one of a considerable amount of capital. Of all immigrant groups, Iranians perhaps have made the greatest investments in America. Herein lies the supreme irony of the closing decade of America's post–World War II imperial claim over Iran: Iran's loss ultimately turned out to be America's gain.

Iranians do not have a history of large-scale emigration. It seems that Iran's role in history, dictated by its geographic location and long-standing cultural solidarity that has sustained

This chapter is based on a portion of a broader 1985–1989 participant observer study and survey of 310 Iranians in Washington, DC, Los Angeles, Seattle, Albuquerque, and New York/New Jersey.

Persia through the ages, weighs against group emigration. (In Persian literature one who leaves home behind [*tark-i-yar va diyar*] has no honored status among his or her people.) Throughout Iranian history, despite the historical continuity of oppressive situations, only one instance of group emigration can be found. In the seventh century a large number of Zoroastrians faithful to the ancient Persian religion emigrated to India, settled particularly in the area of Bombay, and formed the Parsi (Persian) community.

Emigration from Iran to the United States is a recent phenomenon and became significant only in the early 1980s. It occurred during two phases. The first phase started in the 1950s and lasted until 1977. During this period Iranians came often as sojourners and temporary migrants (students, interns) but eventually changed their status to permanent residents. During the peak period (1842–1903) of immigration to the United States, only 130 Iranian nationals were known to have entered America. However, starting in 1945 emigration from Iran rose steadily and in 1966 exceeded 1,200 per year. A peak was reached in 1972 with 3,059 immigrants. The number of nonimmigrants (visitors, students, interns, and so on) increased drastically from an annual average of about 1,400 in the 1950s to 6,000 in the 1960s, reaching the highest figure of 98,018 in 1977. However, during the same period a total of only 34,855 Iranian immigrants were admitted, and 8,877 became naturalized U.S. citizens (Bozorgmehr and Sabbagh, 1988).

It is of particular note that the pattern of Iranian migration during this period did not involve "chain migration"; it was basically an individual migration from a different perspective. It was, in fact, a problem of "brain drain"—the migration of highly intellectual and professional groups (physicians, dentists, scientists, engineers, and so on) to the United States. For instance, from 1962 to 1969 Iran lost to America about 400 physicians and 10,000 other professionals (U.S. Immigration and Naturalization Service [INS], 1985). In the mid–1970s there were 2,373 physicians of Iranian origin on the rolls of the American Medical Association.

The majority of these immigrant Iranian professionals had voluntarily chosen migration as a response to their political, social, and professional marginality in their homeland. At the same time, their feeling of marginality or alienation in Iran co-existed with the experience of cultural estrangement in the United States. As Everett Stonequist once observed, "The individual who has emigrated from the higher classes of a nationality with a proud and self-conscious history finds it especially difficult to identify himself with the new country" (Stonequist, 1937: 88). Thus the tendency toward reemigration was one of the main characteristics of this type of higher class immigrant. Although no accurate official estimates are available with regard to reemigration of Iranian professionals during and after the 1979 revolution, there is evident a relatively sizable number of American-trained returnees now in Iran.

POSTREVOLUTIONARY IRANIAN EMIGRATION

The second phase of Iranian migration began from 1978 to 1980, during the period immediately before and after the Iranian revolution. Insofar as the revolution ousted the Pahlavi dynasty, displaced the ruling class directly associated with it, and established itself as an Islamic republic, it drastically changed the pattern and the nature of Iranian migration. What was once basically an emigration of a limited number of nonreturnee professionals is now predominantly an emigration of a relatively large number of middle- and upper-class Iranian families.

The number of Iranian immigrants has increased dramatically in the 1980s. Estimates of the number of Iranian Americans today vary, with some sources claiming the number exceeds 500,000. Based on most statistical analyses, the Iranian population of the United States grew rapidly to at least 121,000 in 1980 and may well have exceeded 341,000 in 1986 (Bozorgmehr and Sabbagh, 1988). We shall have to await the results of the 1990 Census to determine the precise number of first- and second-generation Iranian Americans today.

Obviously, unlike the prerevolutionary phase, a large number of emigrants are now expatriate Iranians. For instance, during the three-year period from 1982 to March 1985, 18,139 persons born in Iran requested asylum in the United States; of this group, 11,055 were granted political asylum (INS, 1985). Of all nationalities seeking asylum in the United States, Iranians had the highest rate of asylum cases approved—60.4 percent (INS, 1985).

General Pattern

Recent Iranian immigrants are a more heterogeneous group than earlier Iranian emigrants. As for religious affiliation, this exodus includes higher proportions of such Iranian religious minorities as Sunnis, Zoroastrians, Christians (Armenian and Assyrian), Jews, and Bahais. With regard to Jews, for instance, it has been reported that the number of Jews in Iran has dropped from 80,000 before the revolution to about 30,000 today. The great bulk of Persian Jewish immigrants primarily reside in Beverly Hills, Los Angeles, and in Queens, New York. In terms of professional and occupational status, the recent arrivals are mostly academicians, doctors, lawyers, managers, teachers, engineers, entrepreneurs, artists, writers, filmmakers, journalists, former army officers, merchants, and administrators. However, they possess the highest representatives of professional and business categories.

In terms of socioeconomic status, three broad categories account for over 90 percent of the new immigrants: traditional bourgeoisie (for example, *bazaais* or merchants), new middle class (professionals, intellectuals, technocrats), and upper class.

Obviously, the most distinctive feature of the Iranian postrevolutionary migration is its middle- and upper-class character. Unlike the immigrants who came between 1950 and 1978, a large number of new immigrants are upper- and middle-class entrepreneurs and professionals. Thus, the sharp demographic and social composition contrast between the first and second phase is the manifest function of the revolution in 1979, which added an unestimated capital drain situation to an existing brain drain phenomenon.

IRANIAN CAPITALISTS IN GOLDEN EXILE

The Iranian revolution was thoroughly transformative of basic sociocultural and socioeconomic relationships in Iran. However, a large number of Iranian businessmen and affluent families were able to emigrate and still maintain an upper-class lifestyle abroad. This was possible because under the reign of the Shah, dependent capitalism in Iran had developed into a bilocale capitalism. The Shah, the powerful figures of the royal family, and fifty other prominent families who owned most of the Iranian industrial and commercial industries not only kept large amounts of cash in their personal accounts in Swiss banks but had already made major investments abroad.

These so-called transnational capitalists were a newly grown stratum of Iran's dominant class that benefited most of the military group of the 1950s. However, it was during the economic boom and the sharp rise in oil revenues of the 1970s that, at the expense of a national bourgeoisie, they moved to the capitalist rank. They became immoderately wealthy in the commodities market, real estate speculation, large-size agribusiness, finance, and the manufacture of prefabricated parts. Furthermore, the dependency character of the Iranian economy brought these rich families in contact and business association with foreign investors and multinational companies.

No one knows exactly how much money these Iranians brought to the United States, although estimates range between $30 billion and $40 billion. As early as mid–1976 (over two years before the revolution), the British embassy in Tehran estimated that $1 billion of private capital was leaving Iran monthly (Parsons, 1984: 44). It seems that at the time (December 31, 1977) misinformed President Carter was toasting the Shah's regime as an "island of stability in one of the most troubled areas of the world," the well-informed Iranian capitalists had already transferred most of their assets abroad.

With the abundance of petro-dollars, the affluent Iranians had no difficulty exchanging Iranian money for foreign currency. More importantly, the policies pursued by the banking industry, which was ultimately a self-regulated transnational institution in Iran, paved the way for this enormous capital drain. The large credit offered to privately owned firms and factories was often in excess of their fixed assets (that is, plants, machinery, stocks, and so on) to the extent that if these capitalists had to leave the country, they would only leave their debts behind. This, in fact, is what has actually taken place in Iran. After the revolution of

1979, nothing except firms in debt and deserted bankrupt plants remained as the main industrial sectors of the economy (Amir Arjomand, 1984: 111).

Such circumstances and mechanisms explain why upon their arrival in the United States, these Iranian immigrants found for themselves images such as "money refugees," "super-rich Iranians," "Iranians with suitcases full of money," and many other reported stories that were good material for the television talk shows and comedy shows.

In fact, it did not take long before certain expensive areas in Beverly Hills, Santa Monica, San Francisco, Orange County, and even Vancouver, Canada were identified by the local residents as "Persian Hills" or "Iranian mansions," and "Irangeles." Through this visible capital exodus, a number of these rich Iranian immigrants received local and national attention, particularly such extravagances as one-half- to one-million-dollar wedding ceremonies.

In addition to those rich Iranians who have established themselves in America as big real estate owners or successful businessmen, there are other subgroup Iranian immigrants who can be called "unlisted prominent Iranian families in America."

The Iranian hidden community in America consists of both capitalist and noncapitalist elites. It consists of the Shah's son, the royal family, three former prime ministers, and perhaps over 500 former politicians and officials who have secluded themselves to avoid unnecessary publicity. They generally have kept a very low social and political profile since they came to the United States. Only a handful of relatives and close friends have firsthand knowledge of their situation. It seems that there are two main reasons for this self-seclusion and anonymity. One is, understandably, for safety and self-protection against real and potential enemies. Another is to avoid social gatherings in which they are undoubtedly blamed for causing the monarchy to fall.

Wherever the rich Iranian immigrants live today in America, they represent the most impressive example of Iran's big spenders, newly rich and definitely upscale entrepreneurs. They are most likely naturalized Americans but, more importantly, are top-notch American entrepreneurs who have quickly found a niche in the American capitalistic system.

IRANIAN PROFESSIONAL-INTELLIGENTSIA IN EXILE

The majority of Iranian American professionals—such as doctors, scientists, engineers, and technocats who are educated in America—have been able to operate competitively within the open market upon their return to the United States as immigrants. Thus, in terms of professional choice and residential patterns, they resemble more second- and third-generation American-born immigrants rather than first-generation immigrants. In most cases the geographical distribution is determined by either their former institutional affiliation such as hospitals and universities or by their business ties and the nature of their training. For example, hundreds of technicians and engineers who were employed by Iran Air in Iran are now working for Boeing in Seattle. Over 100 top scientists and engineers who had years of experience in Iran's IBM and other electronic industries are now employed by AT&T in New Jersey. Also, hundreds of top engineers of the oil company in Iran, upon arrival in the United States, were able to find jobs in the oil refineries in Houston. In yet another area, the Association of Professional Iranians in the San Francisco Bay area reports that over 5,000 Iranian engineers are working in high-tech companies in the area.

The only group of educated Iranians unable to follow their own line of training in the United States is the former army officers. This subgroup's entry into the American occupational structure has been marked by downward mobility and some disappointments. These Iranian émigrés are well educated by Iranian standards, but after a lifetime of military service they are now driving cabs or managing their own small stationery shops. According to my investigations, most of these displaced Iranians in their new jobs and trades exhibit a work ethic that reduces the exalted Protestant ethic to indolence.

Perhaps the most difficult experience for these exmilitary individuals is the necessity of overcoming a loss of social and economic status. This loss of status is not an easy matter for persons brought up in a status-conscious country like Iran, which placed a high value on position and rank.

In one respect, however, the majority of these nonbourgeoisie middle-class immigrants are in agreement on one issue: America is their land of opportunity, and Iran remains their spiritual land. Just like other Iranian immigrants, they were forced to come here but now they choose to become Americans.

Among the postrevolutionary immigrants, the intelligentsia—whether professionals, writers, poets, artists, journalists, or retired government employees—lives, in a sense, a life in exile. A great number of these individuals who came to the United States because of the revolution would otherwise never have entertained the notion of immigrating from Iran. The intelligentsia in exile is in fact a culture in exile.

Presently, a total of 100 Iranian periodicals including 20 newspapers and 50 journals of various political persuasions are published in the United States. Their commitment to the role of national spokesmen has enabled Iranian writers, filmmakers, and other intelligentsia to produce cultural works of good quality. Iranians in American can thus read today the books of their country's best writers, and they can see the films and plays of outstanding Iranian directors. Unlike most of the Iranian capitalists who quickly assimilated and established themselves here as permanent residents, the intelligentsia are just lately displaying the end of the diaspora mentality. Passage of time and, more importantly, the cultural transformation of postrevolutionary Iran are indicating to them that they cannot go home again.

As the most conscious cultural agents of Iran, they also constitute the most politically minded Iranians in America. In terms of political orientations, the broad category of intelligentsia includes postrevolutionary alienated intellectuals, both Marxists and neo-Marxists. The majority of the 11,055 Iranians granted political asylum during the early 1980s were among those most actively anti-Shah or anti–Islamic republic. A large number of them had been exposed to terror. If not tortured themselves, they may have witnessed it or lost loved ones to the violence of the revolution and its aftermath.

The history of Iranian intellectuals, particularly foreign-educated ones, could very well be written as a history of alienation and political marginality. This is the second time in less than thirty years that the same generation of Iranian intelligentsia was forced to choose between home and exile. The first time was during the early 1960s when the Shah proposed a number of reformist acts and called it a "white revolution" (achievement without bloodshed). In a public speech, the Shah ordered the political opposition and intellectuals either to accept the revolution and join his political party or else leave the country. During the same period, many Iranian students in the United States became politically active against the Shah and thus made themselves self-exiled.

Ironically, the very revolution that brought self-exiled Iranians back home has again forced them to return to exile. The fact that some Iranian political immigrants have chose their "enemy" as their host has created a peculiar, unique situation. In disagreement with both political systems—at home and in the host country—this type of immigrant finds himself or herself in a situation of dual political marginality.

The basic difference between today's situation and that of early 1960s is that the political immigrants have, at the present time, a "mission" orientation. However, the mission orientation has not functioned as a strong organizational principle. The so-called political groups have remained hopelessly divided and fragmented. The promonarchy exiles resemble in some respects those Cuban refugees who came to the United States with the hope of someday overthrowing the Castro regime and returning to Cuba. However, the radical Iranians, who for the second time have chosen their erstwhile "enemy" as their host, are the most disenchanted of the Iranian political immigrants.

THE MAKING OF THE IRANIAN COMMUNITY

Today more Iranians live in the United States than in any other country in the world. U.S. Iranian professionals, more than any other occupational category, comprise the largest segment of Iranians outside of Iran. The typical Iranian immigrant possesses a college degree, an urban life experience, and a greater familiarity with a *Gesellschaft* type of society. According to a U.S. Bureau of the Census report on the foreign-born in the United States, 43 percent of the Iranian-born are college graduates (Supplementary Report, 1984). That is almost triple the 16 percent of all foreign-born and native-born Americans who are college graduates. Of the Iranians working, fully 26 percent are professionals. That is more than double the 12 percent of the native-born and foreign-born (INS, 1985).

Almost two-thirds—64 percent—of all the Iranians in America are men, meaning there are almost two Iranian men for each Iranian woman. Yet among all the foreign-born, less than half—47 percent—are men. Most Iranians are of working age. Only 11 percent are under age 15, compared to 24 percent of the native-born population. A mere 3 percent of Iranians are over age 64, compared to 11 percent of the native-born (INS, 1985).

In terms of geographical distribution, Iranians reside in and around the nation's fourteen major urban areas in the far west and northeast. According to the 1980 Census, 40.4 percent of the Iranian-born live in California, versus 25 percent of all the foreign-born and 10 percent of the native-born. After California, the second largest concentration of Iranians is in New York and New Jersey, and the third largest is in the District of Columbia, Virginia, and Maryland area.

New Community Structures

Since the Iranian revolution in 1978, Iranians in the United States have been transformed from am ambivalent immigrant group of perhaps 80,000 permanent residents and students, scattered and isolated from each other, into an ethnic community of over 500,000 persons, concentrated in communities or "Little Persias."

These new ethnic communities are based on both cultural symbols as well as modern and rational considerations. Iranian immigrants belong to a whole generation of upwardly mobile, secularized cosmopolitans. Unlike the "tired and poor," uneducated refugees of *Gemeinschaft*-type communities, Iranians are professionals, entrepreneurs, well traveled, and bilingual. Therefore, the contents of their cultural baggage often include

American educational degrees, professional licenses, check-books, credit cards, an international driver's license (in the case of absentee American "permanent residents," an expired American driver's license and social security ID), a copy of the *Rubaiyat* of Omar Khayyam, the *shahnameh* (the Persian national epic completed about 1000 A.D.), a piece of Persian miniature, a *Koran* (if he or she is a *shia*), cans of golden caviar, and most definitely packages of Persian pistachio and saffron. Needless to say, some Persian luxury articles such as Persian rugs (Kashan or Kerman made) and other handicraft essentials to decorate his or her Persian room here in America are usually sent separately. All of these material cultural items are either manmade symbols of a unique cultural inheritance or byproducts of Iranian westernization—some say overwesternization—and its Western-educated middle classes.

These new immigrants are indeed ethnic, but they do not live within the traditional communities based on intense, face-to-face, significant, and lasting relationships. They were born and raised in an environment in which their traditional cultural patterns were already undermined. Thus, their communal relationships lack territorial identity and *Gemeinschaft* relationships. As high status ethnics, they don't need their own colony to function as a bridge of transition or a halfway house on the road to assimilation.

This is not to suggest, however, that Iranians in the United States are already structurally assimilated and soon will disappear as Iranians. Indeed, Iranians have just started to create their own communal structure and are displaying a renewed interest in their ethnicity. But, as Max Weber emphasized, the ethnic community itself is not a community; it facilitates types of communal relationships. In that sense Iranians are making their community. Ironically, even though these new organizations are rationally constructed and bureaucratically managed, they respond to the emotional needs of the vast majority of Iranians in America who find themselves dually marginal people. The dialectically interrelated antiwestern action in Iran and anti-Iranian reaction in America not only transferred the already available marginal identity to a much larger group but also reinforced the development of a new community.

The Iranian communities in America are based on nontraditional foundations found in an urban, bureaucratized America. For many Iranian immigrants, these new associations or renovated cultural symbols provide sources for expression of their ethnic identity. Since the second-generation Iranian is rapidly Americanizing, all these institutions in their present content and form are probably one-generation institutions. At the present time, they are the functional equivalent of the immigrant's traditional myths, values, and familiarities. The Iranian immigrants' institutional supports in the American society are: the *Iranian Directory Yellow Pages*, Farsi media, cultural associations, professional associations, *Dowreh* (informal small group alliances), poetry reading night, Persian music concerts, *Khaneghah* (Sufi center), spring and winter festivals, and *masjid* (mosque).

The Iranian Directory Yellow Pages

Ethnic identity in a new country is maintained in various ways. The Iranian community manifests peculiarities derived from its predominantly professional origin, business class, and geographical dispersion. The *Iranian Directory Yellow Pages* is perhaps the closest evidence of a rational, formalized community structure. The establishment of the directory paralleled the arrival of the postrevolutionary Iranian immigrants in America. It was first published in January 1981 in Los Angeles by a young civil engineer. Today there are five *Iranian Directory Yellow Pages* published in the United States: Eastern United States (New York, New Jersey, Connecticut); northern California; southern California; Houston, Texas; and Atlanta, Georgia. The directories, with tens of thousands of listings, are delivered free of charge to Iranian community residents and businesses. Each directory covers the entire nonterritorial professional and business community in the area.

Ketab Corporation, the publisher of the Southern California directory, the largest one, is more than just a publisher. It also owns one of the few Farsi bookstores in America. The bookstore is located on Westwood Boulevard in Los Angeles and is a focal point of the Iranian community. In addition, Ketab Corporation since 1987 has established the only Iranian information center in America. It is called 08 Center, and it is a twenty-four-hour service. The code 08 is the Farsi version of Tehran's old telephone information center. A toll-free call will provide information about businesses and services, cultural and social events in town, books, writers and poets, and welfare and humanitarian agencies. Since 1980, its Yellow Pages have created not only an Iranian version of *buzaare* (the word *bazaar* is a Farsi word meaning traditional market) but also a media identity for the Iranian occupational community.

However, a sociological analysis of the organizational culture of this Iranian marketing firm reveals some distinctive cultural patterns. Its most distinctive feature is its quick success in becoming accepted as trustworthy. This is significant, considering the feeling of insecurity and suspicion that Iranian immigrants brought with them from an oppressive society. In the Iranian community where most people preferred to be known only by their first names and previously gave no information to any institution, Ketab has succeeded in gaining the people's trust.

The directory lists every single occupation and professional service but does not list residence phones. This again is indicative of Iranians' desire to maintain a highly private life and unlisted residencies. Also the directory is bilingual, but out of 848 pages only 13 pages are in English and the rest are in Farsi. Since the Iranian population in the United States is young (according to my sample 35 percent of the population is under 15 years of age) and the majority are unable to read Farsi, the directory will soon become useless unless it accepts Americanization of language (using only English) and remains ethnic only in terms of content and not form.

Farsi Media

The Farsi mass media include newspapers, magazines, radio, television, monthly journals, and books. All are in the Farsi language, except for two journals printed in English.

Today there are a great number of newspapers and magazines aimed at the Iranian community. For instance, five daily newspapers, three magazines, and over ten monthly journals are published in Los Angeles. In fact, there are more Iranian newspapers per capita in America than in Iran. In addition, there are over twenty radio and ten television broadcasts in Farsi in some of the nation's metropolitan areas. Book publishing in Farsi is also a growing phenomenon in the Iranian community in America. In 1989 alone, over twenty new books in Farsi and ten books in English have been advertised and reviewed by the Iranian newspapers. Out of the thirty books published, twenty books were published and even distributed by the authors themselves.

It is important to stress that the Farsi media in the United States is basically a media in exile. It is the only cultural institution that totally emigrated from Iran since the revolution of 1979. Thus, it lacks the historical development of starting as an immigrant media and growing into an American ethnic media. In most cases, these are the same newspapers and magazines that were banned under Iran's Islamic Republic. Just as the Iranian community primarily consists of Iranian-born members with interests and needs of high status immigrants, so its media is also owned and managed by those individuals who were born and trained in Iran.

To the inside observer, the Farsi media appears to be a cultural product imprinted by immigrants' political groups so totally as to show no sign of deculturation. Many of the present-day publications are edited by Iranian-born editors who maintain a mission orientation and appeal to a more unassimilated reader. Those politically oriented media, particularly those that are affiliated with major political groups, are losing their own audiences and readership. On the one hand, the exile community is becoming politically frustrated and retired; on the other hand, the Iranian community in general is becoming younger and consequently only an English-speaking community. Indeed, the prime reality that threatens the Farsi media is the discontinuity of Farsi language among the Iranians in America.

Despite these structural strains, the Farsi media plays a major role in creating an ingroup feeling among Iranians, particularly the postrevolutionary immigrants. In the absence of any other supportive institution to serve as an ethnic center, the Farsi media provides the primary component of Iranian identity. Furthermore, to a significant degree, its Farsi language functions as the only symbolic vehicle for entertainment among Iranians scattered throughout the country.

In fact, newspaper readership in the Iranian community is actually declining in contrast with the increase in the Iranian population in America. Despite the fact that the postrevolutionary immigrants brought to the United States their own media, the Iranian community in general is a consumer of the American media. Based on my own observations, two different factors are involved in such lack of interest. First, the Farsi media in America reflect the realities of the Iranian community. They maintain an outsider position and represent their own factional ideas and political agenda. Second, there is far greater competition for leisure time. The English-language press, radio, and television broadcasts, high frequency of long-distance calls, and the increasing American media's coverage of Iranian affairs all compete for time in the Iranian home in America.

Cultural Associations

Since 1980 a large number of *Anjomans* (associations) have been established that relate directly to the revolution in Iran. From the very beginning of Iranian organized life in America to the 1979 revolution in Iran, there was one major organization that dominated Iranian communal life: the Iranian Student Association (ISA), founded in 1953. Involved in anti-Iranian government activities, it was not appealing to the large nonpolitical community. Not until the revolutionary movement of 1978–1979 did the ISA bring Iranians in America together as it became an outpost of the Iranian revolution.

The study of associational life of Iranian Americans reveals that, among their numerous political and nonpolitical organizations, the most active are the cultural associations. In a highly politicized and hopelessly divided community, the cultural associations with their nonpolitical, nonreligious character, and, more importantly, with their democratic bylaws, have a capacity to attract the majority of Iranians regardless of their political orientations and their religious affiliations.

However, it is important to stress that these cultural associations are basically responding to the interests and needs of the Iranian immigrant. Lectures, social events, music, and even publications are in Farsi. Unlike other second-generation ethnic groups in America, second-generation Iranians are born into families in which the level of material wealth, the area of residence, and the pattern of consumption are the same as that of professional Americans. Thus, lack of physical proximity and social interaction with a large number of other Iranians and greater exposure to the American culture have made the second-generation Iranians quite alien to their parents' cultural associations.

Professional Associations

The increase in professional associations is remarkable, with no parallel in the past. Since the idea of returning to Iran is no longer a dominating element with the majority of immigrants, they now commonly believe that organizational affiliation is essential for an individual's advancement and adjustment.

In my earlier study (Ansari, 1977) 90 percent of the respondents said they had no membership in any professional associations. Among the Iranian physicians no one had any need for an association of Iranian physicians in the United States. Today over 3,000 Iranian physicians are members of the American Medical Association. About 90 percent of other professionals such as scientists, engineers, and managers in my sample are affiliated with different kinds of professional groups. In fact, because of the relative concentration of Iranian professionals in various institutions, they are increasingly becoming occupationally organized.

Presently, the most active professional organization is the Alumni Association of Shiraz University School of Medicine in Iran. It holds annual meetings and sponsors a New Year's Party in New York. At its 1989 annual meeting in Secaucus, New Jersey, it included two Farsi speakers discussing cultural difficulties of Iranians in exile. No Farsi speaker was on the program at all for the 1988 meeting. This growing interest in becoming ethnically American and accepting America as home is the working out of a process that was reinforced by the revolutionary movement of 1978–1979.

Dowreh (Informal Association)

Dowreh consists of an informal group of contemporaries and families who meet on a regular basis, rotating the meeting place among homes of members. Dowreh usually exists within leisure time because the participants are occupationally heterogeneous.

Political dowrehs, which were composed of highly politicized elites, have played a major role in maintaining power positions within the political elite. In this context, dowreh is a functional equivalent of the political machine in urban America.

Dowreh is one of those cultural structures that Iranians have reconstructed in America. At the center of the Iranian community are those intimate primary groups that significantly facilitate communal relationships within a great geographical distance. Furthermore, dowreh tends to transform the formal, impersonal, and bureaucratic world into an informal and personal world. Unlike in Iran, dowreh in Iranian American communities is no longer an exclusive male gathering. In all known fifteen dowrehs in northern New Jersey, for example, an equal participation of males and females exists. Furthermore, just as the Iranian community is increasingly stratified in terms of occupations, so too are the dowrehs differentiated in terms of socioeconomic status.

Poetry Reading Night

Another transplanted cultural symbol from Iran is the poetry reading night. Poetry for Iranians is more than just a form of expression; it is a medium and an essential feature of Iranian social life. Even illiterate Iranians know some poems of their great poets, such as Rumi, Khayyam, Sadi, Hafez, or Firdousi, the composer of the Persian national epic, the Shahnameh. There is hardly a Farsi newspaper without a poem from either these classical poets or the modern poets. In Iran itself, even city streets are named after poets.

Since 1984, some of the poets and writers in large cities such as Los Angeles, New York, and Washington, DC, have recognized the necessity of organizing poetry reading sessions. At these gatherings poets of the Iranian diaspora have found a common cultural focal point. These institutionalized social settings draw large crowds of Iranian Americans from the surrounding area to listen or read what these poets have created. In these rather unique cultural events, there is a great deal of intergroup communication as well as personal exchanges. Unlike the *dowreh*, the poetry reading night is not a closed association of a homogeneous group. It is open to everyone with the same interest.

Since there are many conflicting claims in the Iranian community, poetry and Persian music are the only means by which Iranians come together. Poetry also links Iranians with their lost homeland. In this context, the poetry reading is the embodiment of the émigré's psychological needs and the fear that time is running out for the retention of their ethnicity.

With regard to the Iranian Americans' situation of dual marginality—being marginal in the United States and also marginal at home—these social gatherings are quite self-satisfying and therapeutic. Consequently, national pride is never in short supply when Iranian poets congregate. As a result of their idealization of a "lost paradise," they can claim superiority to the rational structure of American society. This in turn makes for a more ambivalent relationship with the present realities of capitalism and materialism.

Persian Music

Another integrating element of the Iranian American community is Persian music. Iran has a great musical tradition, closely linked to poetry and mysticism. Yet after the 1979 revolution, the Iranian government banned music, viewing it as a means of promoting the "decadent" culture of the West. At the present time, only certain types of music are allowed there, and anyone caught in possession of non-Persian music, such as pop music tapes, is treated as a criminal.

The forced emigration of Iranian musicians and singers added an important communal structure to the life of Iranians in the United States. Today there are about ten Iranian cultural foundations and centers whose purpose is to promote Iranian traditional music.

Persian music today has an important place in the life of the Iranian American community and is expressed through youth orchestras, musical groups, concerts, and musical plays.

Sufi Center (*Khaneghah*)

Sufi is an Arabic word that applies to men and women who adopt an ascetic way of life. Sufiism was originally a practical faith, not a speculative and emotional religion. Early Sufis were closely attached to the Muslim religion but emphasized certain Qur'anic terms and verses. However, in principle, the kind of mystical knowledge represented by Sufiism has no place in Islam, because Allah, who is totally transcendental, can have no direct communication with man. Toward the end of the third century, Sufi mysticism became an organized system, with rules and a spiritual director. A Sufi submitted himself absolutely to the spiritual director's guidance as to one regarded as being in intimate communion with God.

A common saying is, "Sufiism is the supreme manifestation of the Persian mind in the religious sphere." Although not all Islamic mystics were Persians, it is a fact that the great poets of Persia, with few exceptions, adopted the Sufi's symbolic language. The doctrine of Persian Sufiism is illustrated in the celebrated *Mattnawi* of Julal-Uddin Rumi. The depth of religious experience contained in Rumi's work is so great that *Mattnawi* is called the "Qur'an in Persia."

Among the Iranians in the United States, there are a large number of Sufi followers. *Khaneghah* (Sufi centers) exist today in New York, Washington, DC, San Francisco, Los Angeles, Santa Cruz, Santa Fe, Seattle, and Chicago. Since 1987 a monthly journal published in London, in Farsi and English, is distributed to all the U.S. Sufi centers.

Now-ruz (Spring Festival)

Now-ruz (pronounced no-ruze), the Iranian new year festival, is the greatest of the Persian feasts and celebrations. It is also the first day of spring—March 21, the vernal equinox—and has great cultural and national significance for Iranians.

As a spring rite, *Now-ruz* symbolizes all qualities of the season: rebirth, awakening, and the importance of family and friends. In popular Persian legend, *Now-ruz* was said to have been instituted by the mythical Persian king Jamshid. *Now-ruz* has a long history: When the Pilgrims celebrated the first Thanksgiving, *Now-ruz* had already been around for more than 2,000 years.

Preparations for this festival begin weeks before the new year actually arrives. Families plant wheat and lentil grains so they will sprout by *Now-ruz*. On New Year's Day itself, one should wear new clothes, exchange gifts, and visit relatives and friends. About an hour before the moment that signifies the arrival of spring, or *Now-ruz*, the family gathers around the *haft-seen*.

The *haft-seen* is a table decorated with seven items, the names of which in Farsi begin with *seen* or the letter s. Among the most popular are vinegar (*serkeh*); coin (*sekeh*); apple (*sib*); hyacinth (*sounbol*); garlic (*seer*); *somag* (a spice); *samanu* (a sweet wheat pudding); and *senjed* (a dried fruit from an Asian deciduous tree). In addition, there should be a dish of *sabzi* (greens), which usually consist of home-grown wheat sprouts or lentils. The table may also be decorated with a Qur'an, candle, and a goldfish in a bowl. These items are believed to bring happiness to every family during the new year.

The period of the *Now-ruz* festivities extends for two weeks. It begins on the last Wednesday of the outgoing year, called *Chahar-Shanbeh Souri*, the Farsi term for Wednesday. The festivities continue until the thirteenth day of the new year (*Sizdah Bedar*—the Farsi word for thirteen). Since Iranians consider thirteen a symbol of bad luck, they counteract its evil by dwelling only on the good. Earth, air, and water are purifying elements that can ward off the evils of the thirteenth day of the new year. On the morning of this day, Iranians plan an outdoor picnic. They also take along the green sprouts grown for the *haft-seen* table and ceremoniously toss them into a stream of water.

For Iranian Americans, the spring festival, especially the *Now-ruz* celebration, is just as joyous a holiday in America as it ever was. In fact, the *Now-ruz* festival is the only time that Iranian Americans come together as a national ethnic group. For all

Iranians, no matter where they may be when the *Now-ruz* arrives, the most important part of the celebration is the reunion of family and friends. However, it is through the spectacular variety shows and New Year's Eve parties that an atmosphere of national identity is created.

More than fifteen major metropolitan areas hold *Now-ruz* parties with hundreds of guests in attendance. In New York, Los Angeles, and other major cities, other parties are sponsored by political activists and different Iranian religious minorities such as Iranian Jews and Zoroastrians. These separate parties illustrate the polarization of the Iranian community in America.

Shab-e Yalda (Winter Festival)

Shab-e Yalda literally means birthday night. December 21 or 22 is the winter solstice and the longest night of the year. Like so many celebrations of spring rites, the *Shab-e Yalda* ceremony dates back to an Indo-Iranian origin when light and good were considered together against darkness and evil. This longest night was thought to be extremely unlucky with evil at the zenith of its powers.

On this special night family and friends participate in the celebration. They stay up through the night, recite poetry, and tell jokes and stories. An important part of the *Shab-e Yalda* is to serve fresh fruits such as grapes, honeydew melons, watermelons, cucumbers, pomegranates, and *ageels* (dried fruit and nuts). These are eaten on this night in a final ceremony of thanks for the fruitful produce of the past year and of prayer for the coming year.

Mosque (*Masjid*)

Iranian Americans are religiously heterogeneous, and a majority of them are oriented toward a secular rather than religious outlook. Among the religious groups, the majority are Shiite Muslims. Other religious minority groups include Sunni, Jews, Christians, Zoroastrians, Bahai, and a variety of Sufi groups. It must be added that, under the Iranian constitution, Bahais are not considered as followers of a religion but rather as heretics of Shiism. Other religious minorities in Iran are granted legal recognition.

Since the Islamic revolution in Iran, a remarkable religious cohesiveness has developed among a segment of the Iranian Shiite Muslims. This revival, unprecedented in the Iranian community, is today an integrated part of the wider movement of Islam in America. Islam is one of the fastest growing religions in the United States, its numbers now exceeding 4.6 million. With higher rates of immigration and birth, together with significant growth of Muslims among African Americans, American Muslims may surpass the number of American Jews by 2010.

Paralleling the increase in American Muslims has been the tremendous expansion of *masjid* (mosques), particularly in New York City, Chicago, Detroit, Los Angeles, and Toledo. About 600 mosques now exist in the United States, many in small buildings, former churches, converted stores, or even in renovated private homes. Multi-million-dollar mosques have been built in Los Angeles, New York City, and Washington, DC in the 1980s. These newly built mosques symbolize Islamic architecture with domes over their prayer areas and two minarets (about 135 feet high) on each side. Although the majority of U.S. Muslims are not affiliated with a mosque, they are nonetheless formidable institutions, the most socially and politically active centers in the Muslim community.

The overwhelming majority of Iranian Americans are so-called nominal Muslims. For them, Islam is more of a cultural identity. They do not take fundamental Islamic rituals (daily prayers, fasting, giving alms, making the pilgrimage to Mecca) to heart despite the fact that nearly all still declare themselves to be Muslims. Religion has become privatized among modernized Iranians, but it still remains a powerful influence on the Persian mind in this country, particularly in dealing with the ultimate question of one's existence.

If religion remains a cultural affair for the majority of Iranian immigrants, for their children, mostly American-born, Islam is on the wane. Evidence shows that most of the Iranian teenagers have received no Islamic teaching. Out of 200 teenagers in my survey, only 6 boys and 2 girls even visited a mosque. While the typical Iranian-American parent has drifted away from religion, losing Islam in the process of gaining personal freedom and material comfort, the typical second-generation Iranian American is growing up irreligious.

CONCLUSION

Some concluding observations may be made about the different currents of change that are still unfolding in the Iranian community in the United States. Since 1980, the number of Iranians in the United States has tripled—from about 121,000 in 1980 to 355,000 in 1989. The Iranian revolution of 1978 drastically changed the pattern and the nature of Iranian emigration and gave rise to a modern, high status ethnic community based on institutionalized rationality of the culturally distinctive Iranian institutions in a secularized, urbanized America.

The newly born Iranian community in America, which consists of a large number of transnational capitalists and cosmopolitan professionals, is an ethnic community of a special kind. Although it is not an essentially territorially based community, through its modern communal structures it provides sources of personal identity and cultural/ethnic cohesiveness in a society in which individualism means everything but the individual counts for little.

After decades of largely remaining uncertain, undecided *belataklifs* (sojourners), an increasing number of Iranian immigrants are beginning to give up the hope of returning to Iran and are becoming American citizens. Today, as "Little Persias" are emerging in America's major metropolitan areas, almost 400,000 Iranians, settled permanently and well established socioeconomically, are making their own Iranian-American history. What is happening is only the working out of a process that started three decades ago.

REFERENCES

Amir Arjomand, Said. 1984. *The Shadow of God and the Hidden Imam: Religion, Political Order and Societal Change.* Chicago: University of Chicago Press.

Ansari, Maboud. 1977. "A Community in Process: The First Generation of the Iranian Professional Middle Class Immigrants in the United States," *International Review of Modern Sociology* 7: 85–101.

Bozorgmehr, M., and G. Sabbagh. 1988. "High Status Immigrants: A Statistical Profile of Iranians in the United States," *Iranian Studies* 21 (3): 5–36.

Lorentz, John H., and John T. Wertime. 1980. "Iranians," in Stephen Thernstrom (ed.), *Harvard Encyclopedia of American Ethnic Groups*. Cambridge, MA: Harvard University Press.

Parsons, Anthony. 1984. *The Pride and the Fall: Iran 1974–1979*. London: Jonathan Cape.

Stonequist, Everett. 1937. *The Marginal Man*. New York: Scribner, p. 8.

Supplementary Report to 1980 Census Data. 1984. *Iran Times*, November 11, p. 1.

U.S. Immigration and Naturalization Service (INS). 1985. *Statistical Yearbook: 1985*. Washington, DC: U.S. Government Printing Office.

PART THREE

PITFALLS AND PROMISES OF GOVERNMENT POLICY

7

AMERICAN INDIAN DEVELOPMENT POLICIES

C. Matthew Snipp and Gene F. Summers

Since the late nineteenth century a stated goal of U.S. policy has been social and economic equality for American Indians. A variety of measures has been used over the past century to hasten their integration into the mainstream of American society. Yet, nearly a hundred years later, how well has this goal been achieved?

INDICATORS OF SOCIAL AND ECONOMIC WELL-BEING

Although once considered destined for extinction, the American Indian population has grown rapidly throughout the twentieth century (Thornton, 1987; Snipp, 1989). In 1890, the American Indian population was less than 250,000; today there are probably 6 times that many. The 1980 Census counted 1.36 million.

American Indians are about evenly divided between rural and urban areas; many are newcomers to city life. In 1930 barely 10

This chapter was presented at the Eastern Sociological Society annual meeting, Baltimore, March 18, 1989; it will appear in James A. Christenson and Cornelia B. Flora, *Rural Policies for the 1990s*, published by Westview Press, June 1991.

percent of American Indians resided in urban areas, compared to 49 percent in 1980 (U.S. Bureau of the Census, 1937; Snipp, 1989). About two-thirds reside in places west of the Mississippi River. Also, over a third live on land held in trust as federal reservations; all but a handful of these reservations are located in the western United States.

Historically, American Indians have been among the poorest of Americans. Table 7.1 illustrates the relative social and economic well-being of American Indians in 1970 and 1980 and compares them to blacks and whites in 1980.[1] Two conclusions can be drawn from the data in Table 7.1. First, between 1970 and 1980 American Indians made significant improvements in several key areas of socioeconomic well-being.[2] Second, in 1980 they reached economic parity with blacks, but like blacks, they continued to lag far behind whites. For example, in 1980 American Indian family incomes were only 66 percent of the family incomes of whites.

One of the significant gains made by American Indians in the 1970s was in education. In 1980, 56 percent of American Indians over age 25 had twelve years or more of schooling, more than doubling the 22 percent level of 1970. Likewise, median family income in real 1979 dollars rose from $11,547 in 1969 to $13,724 in 1979. These gains were reflected in lower poverty rates for American Indian families, dropping from 33 percent in 1969 to 24 percent in 1979. Other indicators of economic well-being such as labor force participation also followed this pattern of improvement.

In the 1970s, American Indians caught up and in some instances surpassed the economic position of blacks. For example, by 1980 American Indians had a slightly higher percentage (51.2 percent) of persons with twelve or more years of schooling than blacks. They also had slightly higher median family incomes ($12,598) than blacks. Likewise, fewer American Indian families (26.5 percent) than black families had incomes below the official poverty threshold.

U.S. POLICY IN HISTORICAL PERSPECTIVE

Understanding modern public policies directed at achieving social and economic parity for American Indians requires some

Table 7.1
Socioeconomic Characteristics of American Indians,[a] Blacks, and Whites

	American Indians 1970	American Indians 1980	Blacks 1980	Whites 1980
Percent with 12+[b] Years of School	22.0	55.5	51.2	68.8
Median Family[c] Income	$11,547	$13,724	$12,598	$20,835
Percent of Families Living[c] in Poverty	33.0	23.7	26.5	7.0
Unemployment[d] Rate	10.9	13.2	11.8	5.8
Percent not in the Labor Force[e]	50.7	41.4	40.6	37.8

Source: Snipp (1987).

a: Includes Alaska Natives; the U.S. Bureau of the Census does not report this
information separately for American Indians and Alaska Natives.
b: Persons 25 years old and older
c: Income data reported for 1969 and 1979 in constant 1979 dollars.
d: Percent of the civilian labor force without work.
e: Persons 16 years old and older.

knowledge of past policy. Since the founding of the United States, American Indian policy has followed four distinct approaches: isolation, assimilation, termination, and self-determination.[3]

Isolation

Although public policy over the last hundred years has been directed at integrating American Indians into the mainstream of the U.S. economy, it was not always so. Beginning with the founding of the nation, the federal government sought to isolate American Indians from American society. President Thomas Jefferson urged that a part of the Louisiana Purchase be set aside as a special preserve for American Indians. This preserve later became the Indian Territory, in the area of what is now Oklahoma.

President Andrew Jackson proposed to Congress and later

implemented the legislation that profoundly isolated American Indians. In the 1830s Jackson's removal legislation resulted in thousands of American Indians being moved, often forcibly, from their homes in the east to points west of the Mississippi River, distant from frontier settlements. During the remainder of the nineteenth century, treaty negotiations, military action, and federal reservations were used to resettle American Indians in places distant from the newly emerging cities of the west.

Assimilation

In the aftermath of the Indian Wars, relocation, and massive population losses, federal policy moved toward a more benign view of how to fit surviving American Indians into American society. By the late 1800s, it was widely believed that American Indians were on the verge of extinction. Proponents of Indian rights advocated that those remaining should be encouraged to assimilate into the mainstream of white society (Utley, 1984; Prucha, 1984; Hoxie, 1984).

To the reform groups, assimilation meant the adoption of white lifestyles by American Indians. The advocates of assimilation were effective lobbyists, and with support in Congress, the federal government undertook a vigorous campaign to assimilate American Indians. A particularly important component of this campaign was aimed at ending the communal land tenure practices on federal reservations. The General Allotment Act of 1887 (the Dawes Act) sought to create the yeoman farmers of Jeffersonian ideals from American Indians who were formerly communal agriculturists or nomadic hunters (Carlson, 1981; Lewis, 1988). Instead, the male heads of Indian households were allotted free simple title to 160 acres of land, were provided with a few basic farm implements such as a mule and a plow, and were expected to adopt the agricultural lifestyles of their white neighbors (Carlson, 1981).

Assimilation policy was a dismal failure. Fewer Indians were farming and ranching after allotment than before (Carlson, 1988). For lack of experience or fertile cropland, some Indians were unable to become successful farmers (Carlson, 1981). Others, especially those who had been nomadic hunters, simply had no desire to become farmers (Lewis, 1988).

Allotment resulted in massive losses of Indian land, totaling in the millions of acres (Snipp, 1986). Where reservation lands exceeded that needed for allotments, the Bureau of Indian Affairs (BIA) had the option of holding it in trust but often opted to sell the "surplus" land or open it for settlement by non-Indians. Within a short time after allotment, many Indians gave up the title to their land, often without fully appreciating the implications of this act; others lost their land in bank foreclosures and tax auctions.

Recognizing the devastating impact of the allotment policies, the Meriam Report (1928) provided the impetus for the Wheeler-Howard Indian Reorganization Act of 1934, which formally repudiated Indian land allotments (Prucha, 1984; Deloria and Lytle, 1984).

Termination

With the failure of the Allotment Act to hasten Indian assimilation, the Indian Reorganization Act of 1934 curtailed land allotments, returned some allotted land to trust status, and restored authority to tribal governments. This legislation provided a brief hiatus in efforts to assimilate American Indians while the federal government struggled with the Great Depression and World War II. However, shortly after the war, efforts to assimilate American Indians began anew.

The sentiment of federal policy after World War II was to close outstanding accounts with Indian tribes, extinguish the relationship between the tribes and the federal government, and to help individual American Indians move ahead with their lives like other Americans in urban postwar prosperity (Fixico, 1986). These sentiments were carried out in the establishment of the Indian Claims Commission (ICC), efforts to terminate the trust status of reservation lands, and urban relocation programs.

The ICC eventually resolved many claims resulting from treaty violations and broken agreements. It restored some lands for tribal use but more often made remunerative awards for damages done and land illegally seized. However, the ICC proceedings were often highly complex and protracted, with some claims taking twenty years or more to settle (Fixico, 1986).

Termination became official policy with the adoption of House Concurrent Resolution 108 in 1953 that called for the dissolution of the special trust status of reservation lands and the elimination of federal responsibility for this land. In exchange, reservation residents were to receive title to tribal land and natural resources to dispose of as they wished, for example, in timber sales. Termination was to be initiated with only a few reservations and then extended to all reservations.

Perhaps recalling the experience of allotment, many Indian leaders actively opposed termination, and only a few reservations were ever terminated. The largest terminated reservations were the Klamath in Oregon and the Menominee in Wisconsin. In 1975, the Menominee reservation was restored to trust status by special act of Congress, and the Klamath are still actively seeking restoration of their reservation. Of the postwar termination programs, the BIA urban relocation programs were the most active efforts to assimilate American Indians into the mainstream of society. In 1953, the BIA Direct Employment program established relocation centers in a handful of cities such as San Francisco, Los Angeles, Chicago, and Cincinnati. American Indians participating in these programs were provided with moving expenses, job counseling and training, a temporary stipend, and help finding employment. From their inception until the early 1970s, the BIA relocated over 100,000 American Indians from reservations to 10 urban locations (Sorkin, 1978) though the number staying in these locations was probably much smaller. In fact, critics accused the program of being a revolving door for reservation Indians (Fixico, 1986).

Not much is known about the success of relocation programs in assimilating American Indians. There is some evidence that program participants, especially those who were younger and better educated, did benefit from more employment and higher incomes (Clinton et al., 1975; Sorkin, 1978). However, these studies only include persons completing the program and seeking employment in the city. The outcomes of relocation for persons who never completed the program or returned to the reservation are not known, nor is it known how many eventually went back to the reservation; anecdotal information suggests that this number is large (Sorkin, 1978; Fixico, 1986). Furthermore, at least one study suggests that the benefits of rural-urban migration are highly selective and relatively small for the Indian population as a whole (Snipp and Sandefur, 1988).

Self-Determination

The protracted legal struggles in the ICC, the resistance of Indian leaders to termination, and the charges by critics that relocation programs were ineffective at best and a reservation "brain drain" at worst gave federal policymakers reasons to rethink their past efforts to assimilate American Indians. Perhaps bolstered by the civil rights movement of the 1950s and 1960s, "self-determination" became a rallying cry for American Indian activists and their supporters throughout the United States.

The concept of American Indian self-determination was well received by sympathetic members of Congress and by proponents of the so-called New Federalism in the Nixon administration. On January 5, 1975, the idea of self-determination became official policy with passage of the American Indian Self-Determination and Education Act that called for tribal governments to become increasingly responsible for reservation administration. This meant greater federal support for the development of tribal administration capabilities along with ancillary activities such as the development of tribal judicial systems.

In practice, tribes have assumed the management of programs for welfare assistance, housing, job training, education, natural resource conservation, and the maintenance of reservation infrastructures such as roads and bridges. On some reservations tribal governments have nearly complete control of reservation management, while on others, particularly smaller ones, the BIA continues to have a significant role in reservation affairs.

A much broader view of self-determination, one embraced by many tribal leaders, sees in this policy a federal recognition of the political autonomy of tribal governments. This interpretation goes well beyond the mere granting of greater responsibility for administration to tribal governments; it reaffirms the concept of tribal sovereignty (Deloria and Lytle, 1984; Barsh and Henderson, 1980). While it accepts as superior the sovereignty and authority of the federal government, that of state and local government is rejected. However, the exercise of tribal sovereignty is highly controversial, especially since it denies the authority of state and local governments to control, regulate, or otherwise intervene in affairs or reservations.

In combination, the principle of tribal sovereignty and the policy of self-determination mean that tribal leaders are free to develop their community however they please, regardless of state and local restrictions and subject only to federal oversight. According to Francis Paul Prucha:

Tribes can exercise the right of eminent domain, tax and create corporations. They can set up their own form of government, determine their own members, administer justice for tribal members, and regulate domestic relations and members' use of property. They can establish hunting and fishing regulations for their own members within their reservations and can zone and regulate land use. They can do a great many things that independent political entities do, insofar as federal law has not pre-empted their authority. (1984: 1188)

In practice, this can mean the imposition of taxes and vehicle registration and the control of access to fish and game and to recreational facilities. It also gives tribes the right to undertake development projects without regard to locally enforced regulations such as zoning or building codes. A growing number of tribes have taken this opportunity to establish gaming operations, especially bingo parlors and tax-free tobacco shops. The inability to control or regulate these operations, or gain access to the proceeds from them, often outrages local authorities.

The policy of self-determination remained intact through the Reagan administration, although two developments are notable for anticipating the direction of policy in the future. Officially, the Reagan administration embraced a government-to-government relationship between federal and tribal governments (Presidential Commission on Indian Reservation Economies [PCIRE], 1984). However, the administration discouraged tribal governments from undertaking business enterprises traditionally regarded as the domain of the private sector, especially controversial ones such as gaming and duty-free outlets (PCIRE, 1984).

The rejection of tribally owned businesses prompted former Secretary of the Interior James Watt's widely publicized remark that reservations exemplified "failed socialism." Moreover, the Reagan administration supported the passage of 1988 legislation that restricts gaming on Indian reservations. Tribal leaders greeted this legislation with ambivalence; some believe that it is an infringement on tribal sovereignty while others argue that while regulation of gaming restricts their freedom to a degree, it also carries an implicit recognition of the tribal right to establish gaming without state or local government interference.

The authority increasingly exercised by tribal governments has generated considerable resentment among non-Indians, especially among local citizen groups. Many of these groups are pressing for access to hunting, fishing, or other natural resources now under tribal control; so-called equal rights groups are engaged in lobbying against tribal entitlements throughout the western United States. In the state of Washington for example, an active campaign is being conducted against tribal entitlements to a share of the annual salmon harvest. In Wisconsin, antitreaty rights groups are strenuously objecting to Ojibwa spearfishing.

The direction of public policy for American Indians seems unlikely to change dramatically under the Bush administration. Most likely, tribal leaders will continue to push for greater self-determination and tribal sovereignty, while local officials and equal rights citizen groups will campaign against them. The next ten years may hold more opportunities for American Indians than in the past, but they may find their pursuit of these opportunities more threatened than they have been for many years.

POLICY OPTIONS FOR SELF-DETERMINATION

Social and economic inequality can be viewed as reflections of the unequal distribution of ownership of productive assets. These include all the various income-earning factors of production such as land, labor, capital, and institutions. Large differences in the distribution of these factors among groups in society primarily account for the wide divergence between the rich and the poor. Thus, achieving social and economic parity through self-determination requires policy instruments that will increase American Indians' access to income-earning factors of production as individuals, as tribes, or both.

Land

The land and natural resource bases of American Indian reservations vary enormously. In size, they range from California rancherias of a few acres to the Navajo reservation, which overlaps three states and covers an area about the size of West Virginia. Some reservations are richly endowed with natural resources such as mineral and petroleum deposits, timber, fertile soil, and pristine wilderness areas. Other reservations have few, if any, of these resources.

Tribes have available to them at least three alternatives for increasing their access to land and other natural resources. First, they may purchase or lease additional lands for their reservation. This is obviously not a viable strategy for tribes without sufficient capital or income. However, some tribes such as the Wisconsin Oneida have made some progress in planning or establishing land acquisition programs. The high capital requirements of land acquisition could also be reduced by seeking the return of allotted lands through the wills of tribal members and by encouraging the federal government to allocate more public land for tribal use, either through the assignment of title or long-term leases.

Second, greater use of Indian land will require a change in the lease policy of the tribes and the BIA. In the past, the tribes and the BIA have shown a strong predisposition for leasing tribal lands and natural resources to non-Indians. One of the primary reasons for this is that the tribes, and the BIA, have lacked the extensive capital and expertise needed to develop natural resources. For example, tribes with timber frequently opt to sell it to nearby sawmills instead of producing lumber or pulp themselves. Developing mineral and energy resources requires vast amounts of capital, and, to date, tribal involvement in such activities is virtually nonexistent. Nonetheless, if tribes are to receive a greater share of the total value of their resource base, then it is imperative that they become less dependent on lease agreements for development.

Third, for a few tribes, the settlement of land claims and other lawsuits will provide opportunities for expanding their resource base. These settlements surround the enforcement of treaty rights, the restoration of illegally seized land during allotments, and more recently mismanaged and inappropriately leased resources under the administration of the BIA. In some cases, these actions entail small amounts such as a few acres of land illegally seized for taxes. In other cases, the stakes are large, such as in Washington state where the Lummi and several other Pacific Northwest coast tribes successfully enforced their claim for fishing rights and have been able to develop a highly successful fishery industry (Olson, 1988). In Wisconsin, the Ojibwa are claiming treaty rights on fish, game, and timber worth possibly millions of dollars.

Policies for increasing tribal access to land and other natural resources as a factor of production must take into account several considerations:

1. Reservations are not equally endowed, and natural development cannot be viewed as a panacea for expanding opportunities for American Indians. Tribes with little land and few resources will need to depend on other types of development strategies.

2. These resources are finite in supply, and tribes will need to consider carefully not only the rate of their development but methods for managing their conservation.

3. Extractive industries are not only a declining segment of the American economy, they are cyclical and sensitive to economic booms and busts. Tribal leaders may be reluctant to become overly dependent on this type of economic activity.

4. Some tribes may find certain types of land use and natural resource development unacceptable. The disruption and intrusions of tourism have caused some Pueblos in the southwest to be closed to outside visitors. In some tribal cultures, the land is considered sacred, and developments such as mining are viewed as sacrilegious.

Labor

Labor as an income-earning factor of production calls attention to skill, experience, and investment in training and education.

The reservations contain a pool of labor that is less skilled than that of the encompassing counties, although it is by no means an unmarketable labor pool (Snipp and Summers, 1989). The same is true of Indians living off the reservations (Snipp, 1989; Snipp and Summers, 1989). Policy instruments that will improve the accessibility of education and training are of utmost importance to achieving the goals of social and economic parity.

American Indians are divided between those living on reservations and those who reside off reservations. This fact, as well as the failures of past assimilation efforts, must be taken into account in considering options. The ideology of self-determination is quite amenable to both because of its commitment to seeking options that maximize freedom of choice.

Existing legislation clearly establishes the authority of tribal governments to develop their educational systems on the reservations. However, some reservations are limited by insufficient operating funds and physical capital and/or by small pupil populations. Thus, in some instances success of the self-determination policy may require an increase in federal assistance to support tribal investment in its human capital. For small reservations where operating a separate educational system is not feasible, support will need to be provided for off-reservation education.

There are two options for structuring federal support for Indian education and training. One option is to provide the support through transfer payments to the student, the student's family, or tribe. Another is to provide the support through payments directly to the provider, whether that be in the public or private sector. In addition, there is the question of whether the transfer should be tied to the recipient's place of residence. The greatest freedom of choice would be achieved by basing the support on need and permitting the recipient to select the education and training service provider. This alternative has two further features that are particularly attractive. It avoids discrimination between reservation and nonreservation Indians in that place of residence is deemed irrelevant. It permits the recipient to select a provider who is believed to be culturally unbiased and free from ethnic or racial prejudice.

But the mere provision of greater access to education and

training is no guarantee that American Indians will be better off unless complementary policies are pursued that will provide for more productive employment opportunities for those educated. Thus, efforts will be needed to increase the demand for labor, especially through job creation on the reservations.

There is no evidence of any automatic "trickle down" of benefits of regional economic growth. Active and growing economies in the encompassing counties do not result in larger numbers of jobs on the reservations. They do provide some limited opportunities for off-reservation employment but little else (Snipp and Summers, 1989).

Capital

Lack of capital is one reason for the low level of on-reservation development. It is also a contributor to the generally weak multiplier effects of agriculture and other resource-based industries on reservations. The lack of development of consumer-oriented industries on reservations, even those having substantial income from off-reservation employment, also calls attention to the lack of capital (Murray, 1985; Snipp and Summers, 1989; Vinje, 1988).

Ultimately, what is required to achieve social and economic parity for American Indians is their ownership of a proportional share of the nation's capital assets. However, the immediate need is for policy options that will provide them with greater access to finance capital. Two policy options are available to the federal government in this regard. First, it may use tax revenues to finance grants and loans to tribes and individuals for business development projects. Second, it may merely assume the role of guarantor for private sector initiatives to provide business loans and credit. Since the passage of the Self-Determination and Education Act in 1975, both options have been pursued, albeit on a limited scale.

Some reservations are taking advantage of these policy options and are beginning to achieve job creation and capital accumulation (Vinje, 1988). This suggests that an expanded capital fund could permit a wider participation by Indian tribes, business groups, and individuals. One possibility for enlarging the volume of available debt capital would be the establishment of an

American Indian development bank open to subscribers from
all elements of the public and private sectors. If deposits were
guaranteed by the federal government, in the fashion of the
Federal Deposit Insurance Corporation (FDIC), the volume of
available debt capital might be substantially increased. Given
the aim of increasing Indian ownership of capital, policy options
that might encourage non-Indians to take an equity position in
business development on reservations would appear to be counterproductive.

Institutions

Limited experience in business management also limits development. The culture of entrepreneurship, which is so
vaunted by theorists of economic development, is not a familiar
element in the cultures of many reservation Indians (Highwater,
1981). This is especially so if one understands entrepreneurship
as: (a) individual ownership of land and capital and (b) the use
of those resources for personal gain. Communal concepts are
quite strong in many Indian cultures even today. This makes
cooperative and collective ventures attractive organizational
tools for development.

Fortunately, business management skills need not be equated
with individualistic entrepreneurship. Whether the resources
used in business enterprises are communally or privately
owned, their effective use depends on the same knowledge and
understanding of business activities and principles. But given
the cultural heritage of many American Indians, perhaps a better
understanding and application of the concepts and techniques
of industrial democracy would be more appropriate than those
of the private entrepreneur to business development on Indian
reservations.

The political autonomy of tribal governments is in some respects greater than that of municipalities. Their limited sovereignty allows them some comparative advantages. Tribal
governments, for example, can offer outside investors exemptions from certain types of taxes and regulations. However, these
exemptions should be weighed carefully. As David J. Vinje
(1988) points out, there would be no benefit in repealing mini-

mum wage rules so tribal members could compete with 50-cents-per-hour wage workers in Third World nations.

In view of the predisposition toward free-enterprise zones of the past and presumably of the present administration, it seems likely that they will remain important as policy instruments. To maximize tribal benefits from enterprise zones several conditions need to be imposed.

First, implementation of free-enterprise zones must be the decision of the tribal governments. Second, a percentage of the gross business revenues of firms locating on the reservation should be assigned to the Tribal Investment Fund. Third, within a specified number of years (five to ten) no less than 10 percent of the management of each firm should be held by tribal members. The costs of training such management personnel should be borne in full by the business firm. Fourth, the tribe should have an equity position in each firm locating on the reservation. In the case of publicly traded stock companies, this may be done either through tribal stock ownership or individual tribal member stock ownership.

Size of the reservation population also must be taken into consideration in the search for means of on-reservation job creation. It is clear that on-reservation employment is proportionately higher on reservations with larger populations. It is equally clear that many of the reservations have very small resident populations—too small to provide an on-reservation market large enough to support economic development. Yet one must be cautious about writing off small reservations as having no development potential. Family enterprises can be quite successful in creating jobs and can even become large enterprises. Therefore, very small reservations need to consider the prospects of economic development within the framework of small business development rather than regional or community economic development.

NOTES

1. Reliable data for American Indians are difficult to obtain. Unfortunately, the 1980 Census is the most recent source of social and economic data; more up-to-date information is not available.

2. For a variety of complicated methodological reasons related to procedures and processes of racial self-identification in 1970 and 1980, some of the improvements between 1970 and 1980 may not be as large as they seem. Nonetheless, most observers agree that while there were significant improvements between 1970 and 1980, the magnitude of these improvements is less certain. For a discussion of the problems in temporal comparisons for American Indians, see C. Matthew Snipp (1986, 1989) and Jeffrey S. Passell and Patricia A. Berman (1986).

3. This is, of course, an extremely abridged recounting of Indian policy. In reality, its history contains many inconsistencies and complexities that defy simple description and more nearly resembles a record of administrative trial and error with fits and starts, not a simple linear progression (see Prucha, 1984). However, given the limitations of space, we have adopted this four-stage perspective for its brevity and heuristic value even though it exaggerates actors' rationality and clarity of purpose while making history appear to be a monotonic, unidirectional process.

REFERENCES

Barsh, Russel Lawrence, and James Youngblood Henderson. 1980. *The Road: Indian Tribes and Political Liberty*. Berkeley: University of California Press.

Carlson, Leonard A. 1981. *Indians, Bureaucrats, and Land: The Dawes Act and the Decline of Indian Farming*. Westport, CT: Greenwood Press.

———. 1988. "Property rights and American Indians: American Indian farmers and ranchers in the late nineteenth and early twentieth centuries," in Frederick E. Hoxie (ed.), *Overcoming Economic Dependency: Papers and Comments from the First Newberry Library Conference on Themes in American Indian History*, Occasional Papers in Curriculum Series, no. 9. Chicago: Newberry Library, pp. 107–141.

Clinton, Lawrence, Bruce A. Chadwick, and Howard M. Bahr. 1975. "Urban relocation reconsidered: Antecedents of employment among Indian males," *Rural Sociology* 40 (2): 117–133.

Deloria, Vine, Jr., and Clifford M. Lytle. 1984. *The Nations Within: The Past and Future of American Indian Sovereignty*. New York: Pantheon Books.

Fixico, Donald L. 1986. *Termination and Relocation: Federal Indian Policy 1945–1960*. Albuquerque: University of New Mexico Press.

Highwater, Jamake. 1981. *The Primal Mind: Vision and Reality in Indian America*. New York: Harper & Row.

Hoxie, Frederick E. 1984. *A Final Promise: The Campaign to Assimilate the Indians 1880–1920*. Lincoln: University of Nebraska Press.

Institute for Government Research. 1928. *The Problem of Indian Administration* (The Meriam Report). Baltimore: Johns Hopkins Press.

Lewis, David Rich. 1988. "Farming and the Northern Ute experience, 1850–1940," in Frederick E. Hoxie (ed.), *Overcoming Economic Dependency: Papers and Comments from the First Newberry Library Conference on Themes in American Indian History*, Occasional Papers in Curriculum Series, no. 9. Chicago: Newberry Library, pp. 142–164.

Murray, James M. 1985. *The Economic Impact of the Bay Mills and Sault Ste. Marie Indian Communities*. Mimeo. Green Bay, WI: JMA Inc.

Olson, Mary B. 1988. "The legal road to economic development: Fishing rights in western Washington," in C. Matthew Snipp (ed.), *Public Policy Impacts on American Indian Economic Development*. Albuquerque: Institute for Native American Development, University of New Mexico, pp. 77–112.

Passel, Jeffrey S., and Patricia A. Berman. 1986. "Quality of 1980 Census data for American Indians," *Social Biology* 33 (3–4): 163–182.

Presidential Commission on Indian Reservation Economies (PCIRE). 1984. *Report and Recommendations to the President of the United States*. Washington, DC: U.S. Government Printing Office.

Prucha, Francis Paul. 1984. *The Great Father: The United States Government and the American Indians*. Lincoln: University of Nebraska Press.

Snipp, C. Matthew. 1986. "The changing political and economic status of the American Indians: From captive nations to internal colonies," *American Journal of Economics and Sociology* 45 (2): 145–157.

———. 1989. *American Indians: The First of This Land*. New York: Russell Sage Foundation.

Snipp, C. Matthew, and Gary D. Sandefur. 1988. "Earnings of American Indians and Alaska Natives: The effects of residence and migration," *Social Forces* 66 (4): 994–1008.

Snipp, C. Matthew, and Gene F. Summers. 1989. *Jobs and Income in Indian Country*. Mimeo. Madison: Department of Rural Sociology, University of Wisconsin.

Sorkin, Alan L. 1978. *The Urban American Indian*. Lexington, MA: Lexington Books.

Thornton, Russell. 1987. *American Indian Holocaust and Survival: A Population History Since 1492*. Norman: University of Oklahoma Press.

U.S. Bureau of the Census. 1937. *The Indian Population of the United States and Alaska*. Washington, DC: U.S. Government Printing Office.

————. 1983. *General Social and Economic Characteristics, United States Summary*, PC80–1-C1. Washington, DC: U.S. Government Printing Office.

Utley, Robert M. 1984. *The Indian Frontier of the American West 1846–1890*. Albuquerque: University of New Mexico.

Vinje, David J. 1988. "Economic development on reservations in the twentieth century," in Frederick E. Hoxie (ed.), *Overcoming Economic Dependency: Papers and Comments from the First Newberry Library Conference on Themes in American Indian History*, Occasional Papers in Curriculum Series, no. 9. Chicago: Newberry Library, pp. 38–52.

8

AFRICAN AMERICANS AND SOCIAL POLICY IN THE 1990s

Wornie L. Reed

The basic social policy issue for African Americans in the next decade will be a perennial objective: to have policies that will bring them into the economic and social mainstreams of America. The main problems currently faced by blacks are quite familiar: inequalities in economic and social conditions. The new wrinkle in the 1980s was a downturn in racial progress—a downturn that is seen whether one is examining attitudes or specific social policies.

Racial divisions have increased sharply. The Reagan administration's war against affirmative action, its refusal to allow access to decision-making by minorities, its fight against civil rights legislation, and its often demeaning acts and statements about the poor have created bitterness among blacks and have encouraged racists in the white community (Jacobs, 1989: 2).

Against this particular backdrop, constructing the particular dimensions of policies to deal with the situation of blacks in contemporary America is complicated. This chapter discusses issues in economics, education, housing, and health and considers some factors related to developing relevant social policies.

This chapter is a revised version of a paper presented at Eastern Sociological Society annual meeting, Baltimore, March 18, 1989.

POVERTY, EMPLOYMENT, AND INCOME

Poverty among blacks *and* whites increased in the 1980s. Some eight million more people were poor in 1987 than a decade earlier. Two million of these new poor were blacks. Blacks are three times more likely as whites to be poor, and nearly half of all black children live in poverty (Jacobs, 1989).

These shocking trends cannot be attributed to families headed by single females, to the refusal of "lazy" blacks to work, or to generous welfare benefits that discourage workforce participation. The facts say otherwise. Compared with 1979, when black poverty rates were lower, black unemployment rates are the same, and the percentage of the black poor living in female-headed families is lower (U.S. Bureau of the Census, 1989).

On all key measures the economic situation of African Americans continues to lag far behind that of white America. In 1986, the median income of black families was only 57.1 percent of that of white families. This was up only slightly from the 51.1 percent rate in 1947 and was down from rates in the mid–1970s when black family income was occasionally as much as 60 percent of whites (Simms, 1988).

A majority of African Americans in a 1987 survey identified unemployment as one of the three most important public policy issues facing the nation—and for good reason. By 1987 the nation's economy had been steadily expanding for five years, but the unemployment rate for blacks nationwide was 13 percent— almost two and a half times the unemployment rate for whites, which was 5.3 percent (Simms, 1988).

Black unemployment rates have averaged about twice the rates for whites since the end of World War II. Until the mid–1970s the ratio of black to white unemployment had tended to rise when the economy contracted and to fall when the economy expanded. Since 1976, however, the ratio has tended to rise rather than fall each time the economy has expanded. In other words, the gap between black unemployment and white unemployment increases when the economy improves.

The growing unemployment rates of black males reflect to some degree the changes in the nature of the U.S. economy. Between 1940 and 1975 the job opportunities within manufacturing were a major means for black families to move up into the middle-income bracket, as that is the sector that has traditionally provided high-wage jobs to workers with low levels of skills. However, the shift from a manufacturing economy to a service economy is having an adverse effect on current and future prospects for black workers. First, blacks are not well represented in the occupations that are expected to grow the fastest over the next decade. Also, the manufacturing sector has been declining, and, predictably, black employment fell considerably more during the 1980s than overall employment in most of these declining industries (Simms, 1988).

The Joint Center for Political Studies' Economic Policy Task force described four major obstacles to black economic advancement (Simms, 1988):

1. the failure of the economy to generate a sufficient number of jobs for all those willing to work;

2. changes in the nation's industrial structure, which reduced the number of high-paying jobs relative to low-paying jobs for workers without a college education;

3. the limited productivity of many black workers due to inadequate education and training and to chronic health problems; and

4. continuing discrimination within the job market.

THE BLACK MIDDLE CLASS

The continuing importance of race is reflected in all the ways the black middle class suffers in comparison to its white counterpart. First, it is smaller in proportion to the total black population than is the white middle class. Second, it is skewed much more toward a lower- than an upper-middle-class status. Even in professional occupations, blacks tend to be in the lower paying, lower prestige fields, although there have been impressive increases in the number of blacks going into law and medicine since 1978. Third, the black middle-class family, even more than the white, depends on two wage earners. The contribution of the wife's paycheck is especially important. A higher proportion of married black women work than white women, and their average earnings more nearly equal their husbands' than is true in the white family (Pinkney, 1988).

With a more precarious economic status, the black middle class is highly vulnerable to economic downturns and government budget cuts. During the 1970s, the proportion of black workers in the public sector increased from 21 percent to 27 percent, while government employment for whites decreased to 16 percent. The black middle class is also vulnerable to changes in affirmative action policy as affirmative action policy becomes weaker. The number of blacks moving into the middle class becomes less because of this policy change. Thus the black middle class does not have resources equal to those of the white middle class for transmitting its favored class position to its children. Part of this is financial: the net worth of the average black family in 1984 was only $3,400 compared to $39,000 for whites. But part of it is situational: many blacks with middle-class credentials still live in black neighborhoods where they cannot always protect their children from the atmosphere of the streets, the pressure of peers, and the inadequacies of the schools (Pinkney, 1988).

EDUCATION[1]

There is a pattern emerging in American higher education that threatens access to education and therefore to social mobility for African Americans. Since 1960 there has been a definite and significant attainment of educational opportunity as a result of the desegregation movement. For almost two decades colleges and universities were opening admission to substantial numbers of minority students. However, the data show a process of reversal as previous gains in education have been eroding over the last decade. Though the factors influencing this development are mostly systemic due to demographic, social, economic, and policy trends, the consequence has a differential racial impact.

After coming to near parity in 1977, the gap between the rates at which black and white students go to college began to gradually widen. By 1982 the gap was increasing in size, creating an ever widening "access gap" between black and white students. According to data from the American Council on Education, members of minority groups now make up 21 percent of the American population but only 17 percent of college enrollment. However, the patterns vary widely by race. In 1976 there were 1,691,000 minority students in two- and four-year colleges, representing 15.4 percent of all students. By 1984 the figure had risen to 2,063,000 or 17 percent of the total. Black enrollment reached its peak in 1976, when 1,032,000 black students made up 9.4 percent of the college population. By 1984 there were 1,070,000 black students, but they were only 8.8 percent of the total. Between 1976 and 1985, the high school graduation rate of black students rose from 67 percent to 76 percent, while the college-going rate of those graduates fell from 36 percent to 26 percent. Conversely, the high school drop-out rate decreased from 22 percent in 1970 to 12 percent in 1983.

The decline in the rate of college enrollment of blacks is occurring in the face of rising college entrance test efficiency by black students. Recent data from the College Board indicates that the SAT (Scholastic Aptitude Test) scores for black students increased by its largest margin—21 points—between 1977 and 1987.

The figures for students in graduate schools are even more depressed. Black students are critically underrepresented in graduate and professional schools; their enrollment in postgraduate education has dropped since the early 1970s. There has been a nationwide decline from 21,000 full-time black graduate students in 1972 to 18,000 in 1984.

Among the most salient factors accounting for the dramatic reduction of the number of blacks (particularly young males) in American higher education are "rising tuition, declining Federal student assistance, reduced social and political pressure for affirmative action and lack of aggressive recruiting by college admissions staffs" (Pinkney, 1988: 232). Though all these factors are relevant, the most important issue may be financial support. Black youth are more likely to need financial assistance to enable them to enroll in college. In the 18-years-of-age-and-under cohort, nearly half live in households below the poverty line, in contrast to 17 percent of white youth. Most colleges and universities have reduced financial assistance, explaining that they cannot afford to do otherwise because of the shortage in government support for education; federal aid to postsecondary students has dropped substantially since 1980.

RESIDENTIAL SEGREGATION

More than in any other aspect of American society, racial discrimination in housing has not changed very much. Historically, white Americans have refused to live in the same buildings and neighborhoods as blacks, and in some cases they have refused to permit blacks to live peacefully in the same cities, towns, and even counties.

Housing discrimination along with the national urbanization of blacks have led to what some call the development of black ghettos. According to Kenneth Clark, "The dark ghetto's invisible walls have been created by the white society, by those who have power, both to confine those who have *no* power and to perpetuate their powerlessness." He continues, "The dark ghettos are social, political, educational, and, above all, economic colonies. Their inhabitants are subject peoples, victims of the greed, cruelty, insensitivity, [and] guilt" (Clark, 1965: 11).

Similarly, the National Advisory Commission on Civil Disorders, which was established after the widespread destruction accompanying rebellions in black communities throughout the United States in the mid–1960s, reported in 1968 that "What white Americans have never understood, but what the Negro can never forget is that white society is deeply implicated in the ghetto. White institutions created it, white institutions maintain it, and white society condones it" (National Advisory Commission on Civil Disorders, 1968: 2).

The federal government has been involved in housing for nearly half a century, and throughout most of that time the policies of the government supported segregation and discrimination against minorities. It was not until 1962 that minimal steps were taken to curb these practices. Currently, the government, measured by its action during the Reagan administration, appears to be engaged in an effort to dismantle the very legal and programmatic structure by which the fragile foundation of fair housing has been painfully built over the past three decades (U.S. Commission on Civil Rights, 1983: 134).

Discrimination in housing remains pervasive. It is widespread in the rental and sales of housing, in urban and suburban regions, and in public and private housing. Although President Reagan signed a bill in 1986 that strengthened the enforcement of laws banning housing discrimination, the federal government has been far from diligent in addressing itself to housing discrimination. The departments of Housing and Urban Development and Justice are responsible for compliance with fair housing laws, but neither agency has effectively enforced the laws.

Evidence indicates that the residential segregation of blacks is increasing and that they live increasingly in all-black neighborhoods. Between 1950 and 1970, blacks in neighborhoods in twenty large cities where they represented three-fourths of the population increased from 30 percent to 51 percent, while the proportion of blacks in mixed neighborhoods with 25 percent or less blacks declined from 25 percent to 16 percent (Levitan, 1973: 227).

One of the few empirical measures of discrimination in housing is the segregation index. Developed by Karl E. Taeuber and Alma F. Taeuber, the index can be used to measure increases or decreases in housing segregation over time and to compare cities and regions of the country.

The index has been computed for several decades, although the number of cities included in each period varies. The following list presents data on the national segregation index—the degree of segregated housing in the United States—from 1940 through 1980 (Taeuber, 1983: 44).

1940	85.2
1950	87.3
1960	86.1
1970	87.0
1980	81.0

As these data indicate, discrimination in housing is widespread, and there appears to be little promise for substantially reducing it in the near future. It has been suggested that with the six-point drop in the average segregation index for urban areas in the 1970s, "It will take another half century to desegregate these cities. Some cities, such as Chicago, St. Louis, and Washington will take centuries to be fully desegregated" (U.S. Commission on Civil Rights, 1983: 144).

LIFE AND HEALTH

Racial disadvantages in the United States—especially as they relate to blacks in comparison to whites—are nowhere more telling and perhaps more significant than in mortality rates and life expectancy. Blacks do not live as long as whites. In fact, the National Center for Health Statistics recently reported that in 1986 life expectancy for blacks declined for the second year in a row—the first back-to-back annual decline in the century. The black rate declined to 69.4 years, while the white rate increased to a record high of 75.4 years.

Blacks are at higher risk of death throughout the life span, except at very advanced ages. One means of expressing these racial differentials in mortality is the "excess deaths" index. This index expresses the difference between the number of deaths actually observed among blacks and the number of deaths that would have occurred if blacks had experienced the same death rates for each age and sex as the white population. During the period 1979 to 1981, for males and females combined, excess deaths accounted for 47 percent of the total annual deaths of blacks 45 years old or under and for 42 percent of deaths in blacks aged 70 years or under.

Another measure used to illustrate racial differentials in mortality is "person-years of life lost," which incorporates the impact of the age of death on black/white differences. Results indicate that among black men, over 900,000 years of life before age 70 are lost each year in excess of the person-years lost by white men. Among black females nearly 600,000 excess person-years are lost annually in excess of the loss among white females (*Report of the Secretary's Task Force on Black and Minority Health*, 1986a). If blacks had the same death rates as whites, 59,000 black deaths a year would not occur (Miller, 1989).

WHERE DO WE GO FROM HERE?

Race-Specific Solutions

Obviously, solutions to these problems are not simple or easy, but it is clear that policies should be developed to produce better access by blacks to the goods and services of the whole society. Living in a color-blind society is not the way to do it.

Although one can readily understand the desire of some persons to minimize racial strife, ignoring a person's race is an inappropriate means of accomplishing that objective. In a personal relations sense, failing to notice a person's race is not an example of "not being racist." Where vast differences in wealth, power, opportunity, and chances of survival separate the races, failure to acknowledge those differences means that nothing will be done to abolish them. A color-blind social policy in a racist society simply guarantees that racism will be strengthened and perpetuated instead of eradicated.

It may also be misleading to ignore race in examining some indices used nationally and internationally to interpret the status of a population group. The national infant mortality rate has been steadily decreasing: between 1970 and 1985 the rate was cut in half. In fact, it is reasonably close to the 1 percent rate that was established as a policy objective for the 1980s.

Yet the black infant mortality rate is nearly twice the white rate. While the white rate in 1985 was 9.3 deaths per 1,000 live births, the black rate was 18.2 deaths per 1,000 live births. Another way of stating this is that some 1,000 black infants who die each year would be living if the infant mortality rate observed for black infants in a geographic region was as low as that for white infants in the same region (*Report of the Secretary's Task Force on Black and Minority Health*, 1986b).

Although both white and black infant mortality rates have decreased substantially over the period from 1950 to 1985, the gap between black and white rates has increased. In 1950 the black infant mortality rate exceeded the white rate by less than two-thirds; however, in 1985 the black rate exceeded the white rate by almost 100 percent. One of the primary factors related to infant mortality is socioeconomic status; however, there is a race effect over and above the class effect. In fact, the highest socioeconomic status (SES) blacks have higher rates of infant mortality than the lowest SES whites. Moreover, blacks with some college education have higher rates of infant mortality than whites with no more than an eighth-grade education (Reed, 1989).

There is currently an ongoing social policy debate about how to improve the situation of African Americans. On one side is the argument for universality or comprehensiveness; on the other side is the argument for targeting or means-testing (Miller, 1989). Universal or comprehensive programs would be available to everyone, or almost everyone, like Social Security and Medicare. The targeting principle sets out conditions, usually income inadequacy, that must be met in order to receive benefits. Medicaid is an example of this type of program.

The advantage argued on behalf of universality is that it produces social solidarity; it causes groups to join with each other in support of a program rather than dividing groups against each other. Additionally, it avoids the stigmatization of beneficiaries that usually comes with means-tested programs. The negative side of the universality argument is that if everyone is served, there is an inevitable diffusion of program resources, which reduces the ability of a program to aid those most in need.

The assumption of the targeting principle is that targeting benefits provides greater resources to those most in need. The downside of targeting is that programs that are seen as being for the poor, the so-called underclass, and blacks in general face political, financial, and operational obstacles. These are the programs that are most likely to be cut. A comparison between a universal program like Social Security and a targeted program like Aid to Families with Dependent Children (AFDC) is quite illustrative of this point. In the 1970s and 1980s Social Security payments more than kept up with inflation, while AFDC payments suffered losses (Miller, 1989).

S. M. Miller (1989) has addressed this dilemma and has argued that the two approaches should be joined. Universal programs would be the first line of defense. In other words, the needs of the black low-income population would be included as part of efforts to improve the situation of all or most Americans. When this principle is inadequate, then targeting within the universal program would be desirable and effective. In practice then, both universality and targeting would be utilized. The issues would be when and how, not universal or selective.

The Joint Center for Political Studies' Economic Policy Task Force considered several current and future policy areas that could have an effect on the employment and income of blacks. Among these are macroeconomic policy; equal employment opportunity; and education, employment, and training. In their policy recommendations they combine the universal and targeting principles. This group recommended the establishment of a macroeconomic policy that would be aimed at increasing the average rate of economic growth in order to expand the number of employment opportunities available, relying here on the fact that in times of rapid economic growth, blacks have made significant advancements in employment and relative income.

On the other hand, they argue for the government to develop incentives to induce the growing sectors of the economy to employ black workers and to promote policies to make it easier for displaced workers to transfer to new jobs in these industries. Also, they advocate a return to vigorous pursuit of affirmative action policies. This is indeed because discrimination continues to operate in the labor market. Demonstration of this is quite evident in the disparities in employment and earnings between blacks and whites with similar education and experience.

Legal-Class-Specific Solution

Many sociologists who do not think of themselves as working on social policy issues may not see a role for themselves in any of the issues raised in this chapter. Consequently, this discussion will include some related, central sociological issues.

In the *Mobile v. Bolden* case in 1980, the U.S. Supreme Court established a standard that required proof of an intent to discriminate in school desegregation cases. This role of intent in discrimination was supported by the U.S. Supreme Court again in 1982. This situation suggested two points: that the legal process is limited in bringing about desired social change, and the necessity for social scientists, especially sociologists, to add to the public discussion the idea that social processes occur regardless of individual intentions. In other words, racist processes cannot always (and need not always) be explained by individual psychologies (psychological reductionism).

On the one hand is the Supreme Court requiring some demonstration of intent to violate a law before the process can be deemed illegal. On the other hand, sociologists argue that if racist consequences accrue to institutional laws, customs, or practices, the institution is racist whether or not the individuals maintaining those practices have racist intentions. The Kerner Commission Report in 1968 supported this definition of racism. Thus, the law appears to be in contradiction with acknowledged situations.

Of course, institutionalized law—and the Supreme Court— follows social practice. Therefore, social scientists should consider these issues for at least two reasons. One is because this is proper subject matter for social scientists. The other reason is to influence the public knowledge so that the laws might reflect the understanding of social practice.

Another example of the problem that this intent requirement posed was illustrated by the debate in 1982 over the extension of the Voting Rights Act. It appeared that if the Act had been extended in its previous form it would have had very little effect because it would have been subject to the 1980 Supreme Court decision that required evidence of intentional discrimination. Civil rights groups favored the House version of the Voting Rights Act because it required that plaintiffs show only that a local government action *results* in a denial or unabridgement of voting rights. Since a key aspect of social behavior is the insignificance of intent, it would appear that social scientists should have been more involved in this debate.

Although the Supreme Court was using the intent measure in some discrimination areas, three federal appeals courts endorsed the "effects tests" to prove housing discrimination, and no appeals court ruled against it. Prior to the Reagan administration, Justice Department lawyers used the so-called effects tests. These tests permit the department to attempt to prove housing discrimination merely by showing that the decisions of a local government had the *effect* of discrimination regardless of whether the government actually intended to do so. However, the Reagan administration instructed Justice Department lawyers not to use the test. With the absence of any significant and informed protestations from social scientists, the administration was on the way to redefining discrimination such that it may be thought of in terms of legal technicalities rather than social facts.

Fortunately, the Congress extended the Voting Rights Act with new guidelines that make it possible to establish a fact of voting rights discrimination using the "effects test." Even though it turned out satisfactorily, the relative lack of participation of sociologists in this debate is a cause for concern.

Currently, and maybe not so subtly, the anti–affirmative action lobby is winning the day in defining the parameters of this issue. The Reagan administration—including the Rehnquist court—successfully redefined racism as individual discrimination. Now there is little consideration of institutional racism, and, indirectly, remedies are applied to the individuals, not to groups or to legal classes.

Hopefully, social scientists, especially sociologists, will become more involved in the public debate.

NOTE

1. This section is based substantially on A. Pinkney, *Sociocultural Change and Continuity*, unpublished manuscript, 1988.

REFERENCES

Clark, Kenneth B. 1965. *Dark Ghetto*. New York: Harper & Row.

Jacobs, J. E. 1989. "Black America, 1988: An overview," in J. Dewart (ed.), *The State of Black America 1989*. New York: National Urban League, pp. 1–7.

Levitan, S. 1973. *Still a Dream*, Manpower and Policy Studies. Washington, DC: U.S. Government Printing Office.

Miller, S. M. 1989. "Race in the health of America," in D. P. Willis (ed.), *Health Policies and Black Americans*. New Brunswick, NJ: Transaction Publishers.

National Advisory Commission on Civil Disorders. 1968. *Report of the*

National Advisory Commission on Civil Disorders. Washington, DC: U.S. Government Printing Office.

Pinkney, A. 1988. *Sociocultural Change and Continuity*. Unpublished manuscript.

Reed, W. L. 1989. "Racism and health: The case of black infant mortality," in P. Conrad (ed.), *The Sociology of Health and Illness*, 3d ed. New York: St. Martin's Press.

Report of the Secretary's Task Force on Black and Minority Health. 1986a. *Volume II: Crosscutting Issues in Minority Health*. Washington, DC: U.S. Government Printing Office.

————. 1986b. *Volume I: Executive Summary*. Washington, DC: U.S. Government Printing Office.

Simms, M. C. 1988. *Black Economic Progress: An Agenda for the 1990s*. Washington, DC: Joint Center for Political Studies.

Taeuber, Karl. 1983. *Racial Residential Segregation, 28 Cities, 1970–1980*. Madison: University of Wisconsin Center for Demography and Ecology.

U.S. Bureau of the Census. 1989. *Statistical Abstract of the United States: 1989*. Washington, DC: U.S. Government Printing Office.

U.S. Commission on Civil Rights. 1983. *A Sheltered Crisis: The State of Fair Housing in the Eighties*. Washington, DC: U.S. Government Printing Office.

9

MORALITY POLITICS AND U.S. REFUGEE POLICY

Peter I. Rose

"Politics," said Niccolò Machiavelli in *The Prince*, "have no relation to Morals."

To the Florentine statesman, and to many others who have sought to advise others on how to guide the conduct of nations, politics and morals ought to be viewed as separate phenomena: the former being tied to strategies of governing and norms of expedience, the latter to ethical standards about what is right, good, or just.

In fact, what is theoretically separable hardly matters in the everyday affairs of states. Politics is a multifaceted game, and policies carried out by princes and parliamentarians and their agents involve a congeries of factors that invariably blur such distinctions. The moral justification of social behavior is one of the oldest ploys in politics. It has long been evident in the use of ethnocentric expressions like "Gott mit uns," in sanctimonious rhetoric about the weightiness of the "white man's burden," in jingoistic sloganeering about saving the world from communism and other evils. It is evident today in the convoluted newspeak about MX missiles as "peacekeepers," retreaded Som-

This chapter was presented at the Eastern Sociological Society annual meeting, Boston, May 1, 1987. Original version was published as "The Politics and Morality of U.S. Refugee Policy," *New Perspectives* (September/October 1985), pp. 3–8. Reprinted with permission.

ocistas as "freedom fighters," and SS troopers as fellow victims in the Holocaust. Religious and patriotic words that fire the spirit to sharpen the differences between us and them, between in-groups and out-groups, and the actions that precipitate or perpetuate social conflicts belie the notion that morality and politics are really divisible.

Ideologies themselves have a moralistic claim on their adherents, and these infuse and inform government action.

"It is necessary that the prince should know how to color his nature as well, and how to be a great hypocrite and dissembler." There are numerous examples by which to illustrate this additional thought of Machiavelli, but we will consider only one: the treatment of those fleeing oppression and seeking safe havens in other lands, practices tersely but accurately labeled by John Scanlan and Gilbert Loescher as "calculated kindness."

If we parse the Scanlan-Loescher phrase, it will be obvious that the quality of mercy is strained by considerations other than those of purely humanitarian proclivities. Refugee flows are "created" by powerful elements in home societies, some seeking "protection" by banishing those who threaten the status quo, others seeking "purification" by ridding their countries of undesirable elements, or *Untermenshen*. The reception of refugees by others reflects a clear case—or series of cases—of situational morality, too, for it depends in large measure on the relationships those in potential havens have with the sending nations, the current state of international relations, and the vagaries of domestic politics.

The historic record shows that, despite the admonitions specified in Leviticus and Deuteronomy about the "stranger at the gate," regardless of Sophoclean pleas to take in "weary pilgrims," and despite New Testament parables about good Samaritans, wariness of the outsider has been a far more prevalent sentiment in the history of civilization acceptance. More barriers have been erected to prevent entry than bridges laid down to enhance it. Fear of the alien has been a far more common sentiment than compassion. In one of his poems, Rudyard Kipling offered a most reasonable sociological explanation of this morally reprehensible tendency.

The Stranger within my gate
He may be true or kind
But he does not talk my talk—
I cannot feel his mind.
I see the face and the eyes and the mouth,
But not the soul behind.
The men of my own stock
They may do ill or well
But they tell the lies I wanted to,
They are used to the lies I tell;
And we do not need interpreters
When we go to buy or sell.

Kipling was writing of a phenomenon known in Sophocles' day and in our own as xenophobia, the fear of strangers, a much more widely held sentiment than its opposite, philoxenia, the love of the foreigner (which is often translated from the Greek of the New Testament as "hospitality").

If xenophobia is so widespread a sentiment, then how is it that any political exiles have found refuge in others' lands? The explanation lies in the broader social structural context. After all, refugees do not simply appear. They are products of upheavals within and conflicts between societies. Given this social fact, it is not at all surprising that many acts of assistance are offered not simply, solely, or even mainly because of biblical injunction or moral suasion but for geopolitical reasons, with diplomatic points being scored or debts paid or heavy prices extracted for assisting the homeless or granting them asylum.

In this century, the control of borders has become a major social policy issue in many parts of the world. Restrictions motivated by political concerns have greatly complicated already serious social problems in many nations, including our own.

The plight of refugees is a particularly thorny matter since it taxes the consciences (at least of those who claim to believe in the Golden Rule) while making all sorts of demands on the public. And refugee policy—in modern times as in ancient ones—has ramifications not just in terms of international affairs but domestically as well.

In the United States today, the Congress and three executive departments of government are all involved in the making and implementation of refugee policy. Immigration laws, like all others, are enacted by the legislature, but their implementation, particularly those pertaining to refugees, depends upon the foreign policy concerns of the Department of State; the legal authority of the Department of Justice, under whose authority the Immigration and Naturalization Service functions; and the "care and maintenance" function of the Department of Health and Human Services. Through its Office of Refugee Resettlement, the Department of Health and Human Services allocates targeted assistance packages, provides funds to states, lets contracts to private voluntary agencies to provide particular services, and gives grants to refugee-run mutual assistance associations. It also monitors the activities relating to the placement and adjustment of newcomers. These are just the official players in the American refugee/immigration game. The unofficial ones are the members of the public—or, better stated, of the different publics—some represented by powerful lobbyists. Lobbyists today are a recognized category, sometimes organized in political action groups. While such bodies are relatively recent inventions, they have a long prehistory.

Sometimes it is important to remind ourselves that even this nation, which began, in the words of that stirring Thanksgiving cantata, "When a band of exiles moored their bark on the wild New England shore," has rarely treated seekers of sanctuary with equality. For many years there were those who blatantly advocated discrimination against the entry of certain categories of would-be petitioners. There still are.

While it is true that the first hundred years of nationhood were marked by the relatively open entry of hundreds of thousands, there were always concerns about those who were seen as particularly different, as unassimilable. In the early days of the nation there was a tendency to look with favor on those most like the founders, both in looks and in outlooks, and to worry about the others. George Washington and John Adams hoped the newcomers would quickly shed their "foreign ways." And they were talking about people who, like themselves, were white, Protestant, and of northern European background.

The Irish were not welcomed with open arms. Their very

presence evoked concerns about conflicting loyalties; their man-
ners and mores were viewed as offensive. Americans were said
to need protection against such papists, and the American Pro-
tective Association was born. Most of the Irish eventually es-
caped the wrath of the nativists; their rivals—and the rivals of
the new Americans—on the railroads and in the mines were less
lucky. The first restrictive legislation against any specific group
was the Chinese Exclusion Act of 1882. It was a portent.

In 1911, the first Select Commission on Immigration Policy,
the Dillingham Commission, came up with a number of sug-
gestions, all of which reflected the view that too many foreigners
were being allowed into the country, especially those from
southern, central, and eastern Europe. The Dillingham Commission was supported by the testimonials of a number of prominent social scientists. Within a decade the United States was
moving from being a place to which at least the tired and poor
and tempest-tossed of Europe (if not Asia) could find new hope
to an almost completely closed society. The Immigration Act of
1921 established rigid quotas based on 3 percent of the people
who had entered from any given nation in 1910; the Immigration
Act of 1924 reduced the quota to 2 percent and backed the target
year to 1890. These laws effectively closed the "golden door."
Not only did the laws keep out those who were pulled here by
the promise of opportunities said to abound, but they also restricted those who had been driven out of their homelands or
who fled because of racial, religious, or political persecution and
sought refuge in the United States. The counterparts of the Rus-
sian Decembrists and the escapees from Czarist pogroms were
now to be excluded along with the "economic migrants."

Immigration laws had no special category for refugees. Indeed, as David Wyman recently reminded us, the U.S. government would not even make exceptions in the case of those who
sought to escape to Nazi-dominated Europe in the late 1930s
and early 1940s. The Jews who made it for the most part came
under "country" quotas. The rest were abandoned.

Slight breakthroughs did occur in 1944 when President Franklin D. Roosevelt established the War Refugee Programs. But it
was far too little and far too late. In fact, the first American
legislation to deal with such a specific category of individuals,

the Displaced Persons Act, was passed during the Truman administration.

Somewhat of a breakthrough came in 1952 with the passage of the McCarran-Walter Act. Ironically, this came about not so much because of a sudden rise in compassion for the uprooted as a general category but as part of its drafters' concern with the "red menace." Still, refugees finally got their special due—at least some of them did. Refugees were now defined in U.S. law as "individuals fleeing communism," a definition distinguishing them from regular migrants. Only those who fit into the U.S. official profile of victimization could claim, or try to claim, such special status. Under the parole authority of the U.S. Attorney General, thousands of Hungarians, Cubans, and Czechs were able to obtain entry and eventually to apply for citizenship.

The national quota system was finally done away with by the Immigration Act of 1965, a piece of legislation initiated by President John F. Kennedy. But the 1952 definition of refugees remained. Thus, while one significant bias in America's admissions policy was dealt with, another was still to be altered. This was not to be addressed until the late 1970s during debates over an act prompted by the fall of Saigon and the aftermath of war in Indochina.

Under the terms of the Refugee Act of 1980, refugees were finally defined according to criteria nearly identical with those of the U.N. Convention of 1951 and its Protocol on the Status of Refugees of 1967, that is, as those who have suffered categorical persecution based on physical attributes, religious beliefs, or political affiliations or, being out of their countries, have a well-grounded fear of persecution should they return or be sent back. This new definition—new, that is, to Americans—was a major step forward in bringing government policy into line with schoolroom oratory about America as a haven. But, as has been evident in recent years, there remain serious differences in interpreting who really deserves the special title "refugee"; and despite changes in U.S. laws, admission policy continues to reflect some of the earlier cold war biases.

In a paper appropriately titled "The Conundrum of American Immigration and Refugee Policy," political scientist Norman Zucker addresses himself to the paradoxes and pitfalls of some of those recent policies that, to many, are at once too rigid and too flexible. They are rigid, he notes, when authorities wish to stick to the letter of the law, as in the case of the controversies over the selection and admission of young Khmer, or the interning of Haitians in Krone Detention Center in Miami; they are flexible when it is politically expedient to bend the rules, as in permitting dubious applicants from Poland or Laos to be accepted as political refugees rather than as economic migrants.

While allotments for refugee admissions have become considerably more generous in recent years—the United States has taken in over 2 million refugees, including nearly a million Cubans and some 750,000 Indochinese, ten times more than any other nation (save Israel)—U.S. actions in this realm are still essentially reactions to particular political situations. The undercurrent of East-West politics remains the most prominent factor enhancing the opportunities of some and inhibiting the access of others. It is not, however, the only factor.

As indicated earlier, special interest groups have long been a part of the American political scene. Bloc power is an old factor that still must be reckoned with. Generally it is thought of in terms of domestic affairs (such as pressures to advance civil rights, to legalize abortion, to get prayers back in schools, and to provide bilingual education), but, of course, pressures have long been exhausted by powerful constituencies that affect our immigration policies. Think, for example, of how and why amendment after amendment was tacked on to the Simpson-Mazzoli (immigration reform) bill in Congress.

The debates over that proposed piece of legislation offer fascinating insight into general attitudes toward those who want to come to the United States. While refugee issues were far from central to the principal debates on the legislation prompted by the continuing flow of illegal migrants from Mexico, they were not irrelevant. Lawrence Fuchs, formerly the Executive Director of the Select Commission appointed by President Carter, recently offered some interesting views on the latest skirmishes. Included in Fuchs' remarks were several fundamental assumptions by which the commission clearly expressed its awareness that pressures from those seeking refuge would continue to grow and that there was a need to place limitations on in-flows and to set reasonable criteria for equitable treatment. He reports that the commissioners felt that "since these are concerns that are as much transnational as domestic, every effort should be made to seek international solutions." Most pointedly, the commissioners reiterated the view that "the United States would continue to remain a society which values highly the rule of law and immigration policies which are free of biases based on race, color, ethnicity, or nationality."

The bipartisan Select Commission avowed that "the immigrants and refugees who have been lawfully admitted in recent years, as in decades past, have helped to strengthen the United States in a variety of ways—contributing to its economic, cultural and scientific progress." But the members also suggested that "although the illegal immigration of persons may have contributed to over-all economic growth, such immigration tends to have a pernicious effect on Americans and resident aliens [including refugees] who compete with undocumented workers; and the existence of an under-class of exploitable, illegal aliens is harmful generally to American society."

While this sounded most reasonable, the debates in the Congress took ominous twists. In addition to failing to take up recommendations by the Select Commission that would have dropped "crowned colony ceilings which now applied detrimentally to Hong Kong," it did not even consider the suggestion to increase numerical restrictions (legacies of the 1965 Act) and provide a hundred thousand visas a year for five years to clear the backlog. Why were they dropped for consideration? Some argue that it was because these matters, while reviewed by an interagency task force, were not timely, given the "rising negative concerns about immigration at a time of high unemployment."

Fuchs and others point out that although in the Senate the debate on lawful admission increased, the Senate failed to accept the recommendation and voted fifteen-to-one (with Senator Alan Simpson casting the only "nay" vote) that spouses, children, and parents of U.S. citizens and of bona fide refugees resident in the United States can be exempted from targets or ceilings.

The House version came closer to the commissioner's recommendations particularly in regard to family reunification. But it, too, held the line on numbers.

In one sense there was consistency:

[B]oth Houses did follow the Select Commission in asserting the importance of keeping the front door open to admission at present levels [approximately 425,000] . . . , providing for a substantial program to legalize illegal aliens now in the United States [the highly emotional amnesty issue] . . . , [and, importantly, especially given our main concern here] keeping the admission of refugees separate from that of immigrants.

While advocates of refugees and asylees were interested and active on Capitol Hill during the ill-fated debates, none was more involved than representatives of those most likely to be affected by the major thrust of the Simpson-Mazzoli bill, that is, the members of the Hispanic caucus. Included here were a number of people worried about the effect it would have on Central American asylum seekers who entered from Mexico. Hispanic blocs were effective in turning the tide and forcing reconsideration or, at very least, postponement of actions that many saw as racially motivated and that others viewed as dangerous for all who might be viewed as illegals or "undesirables," a word that harkens back to the days of the Dillingham Commission.

The fact is that political constituencies, or what David Reisman once called "veto groups," have significant clout regarding social policy, including immigration and refugee policy. Let me suggest how this is being played out today.

There is little question that some of those who have recently sought admission to the United States have benefited not only by having gotten out of the right (actually "left") place at the right time but also because they have had very strong and effective lobbyists championing their causes, such as those concerned about particular ethnic and religious groups. The cases of those such as Soviet Jews are just, but that does not gainsay the fact that far fewer voices are being raised to assist the Salvadorans or Guatemalans to get out of their repressive societies or to ease their entry into this new one.

There is one other matter. With the exception of Cubans in 1960 (originally admitted under special dispensations) and the Mariel and Haitian boat people, almost all of the others currently designated as refugees have come through other countries, screened, as it were, through a bureaucratic filter that seeks to determine their official admissibility. Like Malaysia, Thailand, Hong Kong, Singapore, Indonesia, and the Philippines, the United States has recently had to face the prospect of becoming a mass "first asylum," where large numbers of expellees and escapees have tried to land. Like other governments, the United States, too, has balked at the prospect of an uncontrolled influx, and so has its public.

Malaysian authorities worry about large numbers of Sino-Vietnamese who might upset the delicate ethnic balance between the numerically and politically dominant Malays and the economically powerful Chinese. The Thais worry about subversive elements infiltrating their society. Many Americans also seem to have their own special concerns. From some there is still that bogey-man image of "undesirable aliens"; for many there is worry about a "slippery slope."

The first concern harkens back to earlier campaigns—nativist in name, racist in character—that specified who should be permitted to enter the society and participate in the system. It was such sentiment that led to the Chinese Exclusion Act of 1882 and the more comprehensive restrictive legislation of the 1920s discussed earlier.

The extensive publicity about Fidel Castro's castoffs, including the small but significant group of criminals who infiltrated Miami's underworld and engaged in nefarious activities as far north as Union City, New Jersey, and the South Bronx, has given credence to those who claim that such rogues are typical of what can be expected if anyone who claims persecution is allowed to enter. As is often the case, many newly arrived Cubans of spotless character have been tarred with the same brush. This makes it more difficult for them to find easy access to the American mainstream and, increasingly isolated, more apt to use survival tactics that confirm stereotypes about them. This is a clear case of the self-fulfilling prophecy: those undesired become undesirable. Similar situations have occurred with other refugee cohorts.

If the first matter is a throwback to reactionary sentiments of an earlier era, the second has to do with the problem that may be an unintended consequence of liberal policies including those advocated by President Carter's Select Commission. Once a person has gained entry into the United States as a refugee, he or she becomes, in the lingo of the Immigration and Naturalization Service, first an "anchor" then a "magnet." Immediate family members seeking to join their relatives have priority. Federal authorities in the Department of Health and Human Services, state welfare offices, and members of local communities who provide sponsorship have had to deal with the escalation of people who often define "immediate family" in far broader terms than most Americans and have had to deal with the extra burdens that are thus created. There is increasing pressure—evidenced in those debates in the Senate—to avoid what is sometimes described as the threat of inundation.

Of late, concerns have also been raised not only by traditional advocates of restricted entry but also by those who might be called "neonativists" of varying backgrounds and political persuasions. Included in the latter category are leaders of some minority communities and the rank and file of various labor unions who, echoing the thoughts of Samuel Gompers and others, once again express concern about favoring the non-American needy while failing to deal effectively with the economic woes of American workers. Worried about the fact that the United States is no longer in charge of its borders and about competition from the outside, little distinction is made based on the motivation of the immigrants, that is, whether they are being pulled in in the classic manner of economic migrants or pushed in and forced into exile.

But even for those who do know the difference or make the distinction, there is still disagreement about what to do. The highly volatile issue of asylum is the largest case in point. A statement jointly issued by the American Jewish Committee (one of the oldest of the "defense organizations"), the International Rescue Committee (one of the principal voluntary agencies that deals with refugee resettlement), and the Center for Migration Studies of New York urged the United States to reaffirm its tradition of rescue, even to increase the number of people allowed into the country as refugees and asylees. Furthermore, the ad hoc group urged government officials to separate the issue of refugees from debates on foreign policy, a well-intentioned but almost impossible strategy to put ethics above political concerns.

The representatives of the three organizations know how biased the supposedly fair policies—now that there is the 1980 Act—actually are. Everyone else should too. A few statistics illustrate this unfairness. In 1984 people from El Salvador seeking asylum in the United States were turned down by a ratio of forty-to-one, those from Nicaragua seven-to-one, and those from Poland two-to-one. As signatories of the joint statement said, "These figures do not reflect this country's deep commitment to freedom or dedication to fairness." Nor does the fact that between 1981 and 1984 the U.S. government deported nearly forty-five Salvadorans, and that was before Jose Napoleon Duarte had received the presidency in San Salvador. If not in direct response to the statement quoted above, it was certainly ironic that, three days after its issuance, the Reagan administration announced preparation of extensive changes in the rules and procedures for granting asylum to aliens. Immigration authorities were to be given more flexibility in handling applications. That was not a good omen. Under the Refugee Act of 1980, aliens could qualify for asylum if they "have a well-founded fear of persecution" in their home country "on account of race, religion, nationality, membership in a particular social group, or political opinion." But, according to a *New York Times* article on March 18, 1985, the U.S. Immigration and Naturalization Service and the State Department began to argue that it is not enough for aliens to show general conditions of violence in their homelands. They must show that it is likely that they will be singled out for persecution. The *Times* also states: "The Administration maintains that illegal aliens from Latin America are fleeing poverty, not persecution, and do not qualify for asylum."

Of course, all of this is related to the sanctuary movement, even though immigration officials say that the new regulations are not part of an effort to curb it. Yet, the leaders of the sanctuary movement themselves indicate that "decisions on granting asylum have become so entwined with politics and foreign politics that they are not objective or fair."

Not surprisingly, difficult choices in refugee policy, as in other matters of moment, are weighed more by political concerns than by ethical or humanitarian standards. There are times, of course, when the two do converge, as in the case of saving Vietnamese boat people. Then, it seems, policymakers, those in the business of caring, and other participants in the rescue, relief, and resettlement chain can be both pure of heart and politically pragmatic. But when moral sensibilities clash with national interests or domestic concerns, the former inevitably seem to suffer.

One cannot help but think of Jeanne Kirkpatrick's distinction between regimes that are "totalitarian"—the sort of systems we love to hate—and "authoritarian"—the kind we hate to love but frequently embrace and support. We have an exciting name for the opponents of the former—those who join movements such as Solidarity; we call them "freedom fighters." Those less active, such as many first-wave Cuban immigrants, we call "victims." But what of those coming from right-wing dictatorships? While it is true—though rare—that active and outspoken resisters like the South African poet Dennis Brutus may after a long period of negotiations be admitted, those less active, such as many Haitians and Salvadorans who, like their Vietnamese and Polish counterparts, would rather live under freedom than tyranny, are not labeled as victims. We call them "opportunists." And opportunists are economic migrants who are supposed to get into the long queues of the American consulates where they may apply for immigration.

Having opened with a quote from Machiavelli, I close with one from Albert Camus. In *The Myth of Sisyphus*, Camus says: "There can be no question of holding forth on ethics. I have seen people behave very badly with great morality, and I know every day that integrity has no need of rules."

Writing about American race relations, Gunnar Myrdal (1944) once said that he observed a great discrepancy between Americans' creed and their conduct. But others pointed out that, at least in certain sectors of our democracy, there was no discrepancy. It was simply that those who saw certain people as inferior held to a different creed. Such selections seem to inform our refugee policy today. The questions, then as now, are: Whose morality does one invoke? Whose politics does one apply?

PART FOUR

THE FUTURE

10

PROMOTING PLURALISM

Joseph Giordano and Irving M. Levine

The depiction of ethnic characters in the media has been the subject of hot debates for decades. The feeling still exists among leaders of many ethnic groups that very little has changed in the negative and stereotyped way they are portrayed. On the other hand, media managers believe that they have become more culturally sensitive and often view the demand of ethnic groups as out of touch with the realities of the industry. The truth lies somewhere in the middle.

Unquestionably, more minority and ethnic characters and scenes can be seen than in the days of "Father Knows Best" and "Ozzie and Harriet." But television programs and films are still marred by the low visibility of certain groups and the stereotyping of others.

While the news media played an important role in the 1960s by vividly documenting in pictures the struggle for civil rights, today too many radio and television stations deliberately try to hype ratings by showcasing extremists and bigots. Their appearance often works to increase tensions between ethnic groups. Today's media are rarely as crude in depicting ethnic

This chapter is reprinted with permission from the Spring, 1988 issue of *Media & Values* magazine: *Ethnic Diversity: Challenging the Media* published by the Center for Media and Values, Los Angeles.

groups as greeting cards and "truly tasteless" joke books, and the stereotypes that occur are presented in a more sophisticated form. Nevertheless, they do reinforce bigotry.

Is change hopeless? Probably not. In spite of this long and somewhat negative history, the time is ripe for positive changes.

Creative cooperation between media professionals and ethnic groups may now be more propitious than ever. The following combination of factors lead us to that conclusion:

- A number of ugly racial confrontations in the past few years—for example, in Howard Beach, New York, and Forsyth County, Georgia—may have served the same function as the urban riots of the 1960s: to remind Americans of how deep the racial divisions are in the United States, how explosive they can be, and the important role the media can play in reducing or enlarging those tensions.

- Historical, sociological, and psychological research continues to show that ethnic ties are far more than an immigrant phenomenon; rather, they help shape an individual's character and personal story line for generations beyond immigration. Conversely, individuals who deny or are cut off from their ethnic identities often suffer lowered self-esteem.

- Whether we are talking about new technology like 100-plus-channel television and VCRs or growing ethnic outlets like minority television channels and ethnic magazines, the growth of the media provides more forms for media expression.

- Mass media programming, particularly television, is becoming more authentic both in terms of the variety of characters shown (as in the colorful ethnic, as well as gender and class, interactions of "Cagney and Lacey," "St. Elsewhere," "thirtysomething," and "Hill Street Blues") and in the presentation of such once-taboo topics as spouse abuse and teenage suicide. As the networks learned in such mini series as "Roots" and "Holocaust," delving into an ethnic group's story can make for programming that is educationally enriching, dramatically compelling, and commercially profitable.

- In the area of news coverage, radio and television stations are becoming more self-critical than in the past, as evidenced by the presence of such articulate inside critics as Bill Moyers and the number of stations that have initiated and maintained regular contact with ethnic group leaders.

- The emergence of a new generation of writers, such as Maxine Hong

Kingston, Richard Rodriguez, and Paul Cowan (respectively Chinese-, Mexican-, and Jewish-American), is providing the mass media with a greatly expanded pool of story ideas. Each ethnic group has a rich history and folk tradition that the mass media barely have begun to plumb.

Both media professionals and ethnic group leaders will benefit if they take advantage of this new climate by reaching out to each other.

For their part, media leaders should recognize that there is a real audience for programs and films that portray a fully pluralist America. Such television series as "The Cosby Show," "L.A. Law," "Frank's Place," and "A Year in the Life," and films including "La Bamba" and "The Color Purple" already show that there is a substantial audience for "real"—stereotype-breaking and ethnically diverse—characters.

Authenticity becomes even more important in light of a 1988 study for the American Jewish Committee by S. Robert Lichter and Linda S. Lichter of how adolescents react to ethnic characters on prime time television shows. They view the characters as typical of the groups they represent. Therefore, television programs must involve not only a certain variety of nonstereotyped ethnic characters but, more positively, characters who reflect the values and styles of their traditions.

Segments on "thirtysomething," "A Year in the Life," and "L.A. Law" deal with meaningful feelings about intermarriage. For example, when the Christian mother on "A Year in the Life" first refuses to participate in the Jewish naming ritual but then talks alone to her infant daughter about her Hebrew name, viewers experience her conflict.

NEW DIMENSIONS

Media leaders generally have viewed ethnic America as consisting of pressure groups. A new, more sympathetic perspective on American pluralism means perceiving its groups as resources, both in terms of creative personnel and story ideas. It would involve reaching out to attract and help train directors, producers, writers, actors, camera people, and other personnel from many ethnic backgrounds. For example, the major television networks and PBS (Public Broadcasting System) might sponsor contests, with significant cash awards, or the best original plays on ethnic America. Schools of communication and film, as well as television and radio stations and film companies, also should consider including curricula on the ethnic dimension of news and entertainment in their base training and continuing-education programs.

The most concrete contribution the mass media can make is to develop, and adhere to, guidelines for good ethnic programming and news coverage. Some examples are to present characters who speak in correct accents, to avoid negative stereotypes (the "dumb Pole," "drunk Irishman," "inscrutable Chinese," or "Italian gangster"), and to cover racial or other intergroup tensions in a way that fairly and knowledgeably covers each side's interests and avoids stoking intergroup tensions. News coverage in particular should avoid giving the most coverage to the most extreme, hatemongering views.

REACHING OUT

For their part, ethnic group leaders also need to adopt a less adversarial stance toward the media. Before complaining about coverage of their group or otherwise engaging in advocacy, they must come to understand how the media work and the complex structural, commercial, creative, and social dynamics to which they are subjected. When it comes to television, for example, ethnic leaders need to understand how many individuals are involved in covering a news story or shaping a series and how the intense ratings wars affect programming. For better or worse, the media are comprised of businesses whose primary focus is what will enhance the bottom line. Appreciating the corporate dimension of the mass media does not mean that ethnic advocates should not, or cannot, influence them. But it does imply that they must develop the interpersonal, public relations and other skills to ensure their being heard.

Part of this process is to know not only when to challenge but also when to support. Rather than simply complain, ethnic lead-

HATE ON THE AIR EXPLOITS EXTREMISM

Bigotry. Hatred. Intolerance.

From shock radio to network television shows, from computer bulletin boards to "dial-a-bigot" telephone services, extremists crowd the airwaves with their inflammatory ideas, and ratings-conscious talk show hosts often egg them on.

First Amendment restrictions prohibit censorship, but such messages of hate need not be tolerated. In fact, they can and must be stopped.

"Surround them," is the message of the American Jewish Committee and other groups, who urge local monitoring and feedback as well as organized efforts to explode prejudice with balanced programming.

Some ideas for countering bigotry are:

- Demand equal time to present your side when groups in your community are slurred. On computer services, provide alternative messages.

- Establish regular relationships with media managers to establish policies designed to defuse on-air bigotry.

- Call meetings between media leaders and representatives of ethnic, racial, religious, and civil organizations to discuss the proper role of the media in dealing with extremism.

- Present program ideas that feature positive and balanced treatment of ethnic and racial issues and local controversies related to ethnicity.

- Challenge the fitness of hatemongers to hold FCC licenses.

Feedback should be presented in ways that do not dignify the agents of hate. But it must be made clear to station managers and others that the public airwaves belong to all people and thus cannot be used to malign ethnic groups under the guise of free expression and to the financial benefit of media ownership.

---

ers should applaud quality programming involving ethnic content. They should do so particularly when a station or film company has taken a risk with material that previously was considered parochial or too controversial.

Ethnic America also has an obligation to promote such risk-taking, to broaden horizons, and to confront stereotypes by educating media corporations.

At the same time, if ethnic leaders want media executives to tap their creative resources, they have the obligation to develop their resources to the fullest. Ethnic groups in America must more adequately support their own writers, artists, and filmmakers. They need to undertake comprehensive, well-organized oral history projects and have at least one museum documenting that group's story in both the "old country" and in America. Many groups do all of these things but do not adequately connect with media representatives who might be convinced to take seriously the material that is available for good authentic programming.

Finally, ethnic groups would comprise a more potent force in influencing the media if they entered into coalitions rather than going it alone. The more extensive experience of some groups (for example, Jews and blacks) in what has been called "the art and science of influence" could benefit other groups, while the strength of *all* groups would be enhanced by a sharing of expertise.

Ultimately, the goal of such coalition-building within ethnic America is not to confront the media but to build bridges to it. Ethnic America and the mass media need each other. Each group in the United States needs to be seen and to be portrayed fairly by the major channels of communication in order to get its message across to the general American public. Conversely, the mass media, which are ever in danger of being stale in their entertainment programming and superficial or inaccurate in their news coverage, need to utilize ethnic diversity as an inexhaustible source of creative renewal.

SELECTED BIBLIOGRAPHY

Alba, Richard D. *Italian Americans: Into the Twilight of Ethnicity.* Englewood Cliffs, NJ: Prentice-Hall, 1985.

Ansari, Maboud. *The Iranians in the United States.* New York: Associated Faculty Press, 1988.

Deloria, Vine, Jr. (ed.). *American Indian Policy in the 20th Century.* Norman: University of Oklahoma Press, 1985.

Kitano, Harry H. L., and Roger Daniels. *Asian Americans: Emerging Minorities.* Englewood Cliffs, NJ: Prentice-Hall, 1988.

Mindel, Charles H., and Robert W. Habenstein (eds.). *Ethnic Families in America: Patterns and Variations,* 3d ed. New York: Elsevier, 1988.

Moore, Joan W., and Harry Pachon. *Hispanics in the United States.* Englewood Cliffs, NJ: Prentice-Hall, 1985.

Naff, Aliza. *The Arab Americans.* New York: Chelsea House Publishers, 1988.

Parrillo, Vincent N. *Strangers to These Shores,* 3d ed. New York: Macmillan, 1990.

Pido, Antonio J. A. *The Pilipinos in America.* New York: Center for Migration Studies, 1986.

Pinkney, Alphonso. *Black Americans,* 3d ed. Englewood Cliffs, NJ: Prentice-Hall, 1987.

Simon, Rita. *Public Opinion and the Immigrants: Print Media Coverage 1880–1980.* Lexington, MA: Lexington Books, 1985.

Williams, James D. *The State of Black America in 1986.* New York: National Urban League, 1986.

INDEX

ABOUT THE EDITOR AND CONTRIBUTORS

VINCENT N. PARRILLO is professor of sociology and department chair at the William Paterson College of New Jersey. He is the author of the leading race and ethnic relations college text *Strangers to These Shores* (3d ed., 1990), *Contemporary Social Problems* (2d ed., 1990), and *Social Problems: Definition, Impact, Solution* (1985). Among his many published articles on immigration and ethnicity are pioneering works on Asian Americans in American Politics and Arab American residential patterning and acculturation. He is presently completing work on *Guardians of the Gate*, a historical novel about Ellis Island.

RICHARD D. ALBA is a professor of sociology and public policy at the State University of New York at Albany, where he also founded the Center for Social and Demographic Analysis. His primary area of interest is ethnicity in the United States, and he is the author of numerous articles on this subject that have appeared in major journals of sociology. His books include *Ethnic Identity: The Transformation of White America* (1990) and *Italian Americans: Into the Twilight of Ethnicity* (1985). At present, he is investigating the suburbanization patterns of different racial and ethnic groups, including those of new immigrant groups from Asia, Latin America, and the Caribbean.

MABOUD ANSARI is an associate professor of sociology at the William Paterson College of New Jersey. Ansari returned to Iran in 1978 and joined the faculty of Reza Shah University. For the academic year 1978–1979, he was the chancellor of North University in Iran. From 1980 to 1984, he was a research advisor for the International Institute for Adult Literacy in Iran. His major academic and research interests include ethnic groups, social organizations, and cultural change, especially cultural changes in the Islamic Republic of Iran. In addition to various articles published in English and Farsi, Ansari has published *The Sociological Imagination* (trans. into Farsi, 1979) and coauthored (with H. Adibi) *Sociological Theory* (in Farsi, 1979). He has recently finished his translation of *Protestant Ethic and Spirit of Capitalism*, which is being accepted for publication in Iran. Ansari is currently writing two books: *Iranian Immigrants and Their Children: Ethnic Identity and Assimilation* and *Revolution and Mass Mobilization: The Transformation of Political Culture in Iran*.

JOSEPH GIORDANO is director of the Center on Ethnicity, Behavior, and Communications in the American Jewish Committee's National Affairs Department. A social worker and family therapist, he was formerly assistant commissioner of New York City's Department of Mental Health and Mental Retardation Services. In 1977, Giordano was appointed to the President's Commission on Mental Health, serving on the Task Force on Special Populations. In 1980, he was elected chairman of the Coalition for the White House Conference on Family, which was composed of fifty-four national organizations. Giordano has written extensively on the issues related to ethnicity, mental health, the family, and the media. His articles have appeared in the *New York Times*, *New York Newsday*, the *Daily News*, the *Chicago Sun Times*, *Il Progresso*, *Attenzione* magazine, and *Ms.* magazine. With Monica McGoldrick and John Pearce, he edited *Ethnicity and Family Therapy* (1982), and he is the author of *The Italian American Catalogue* (1986).

IRVING M. LEVINE is director of the Institute for American Pluralism, which is considered one of America's leading think tanks and social action and training centers in the field of American ethnicity. As the principal organizer and chairman of the historic National Consultation on Ethnic America held at Fordham University in June 1968, Levine foresaw trends in American life that only now have become visible to all. He pioneered a fresh emphasis on the part of intergroup specialists, social scientists, government officials, and ethnic leaders to deal more effectively with the reality of American ethnicity and with new issues of group conflict, group interest, and group identity. Honest discussion of American diversity within a framework of legitimate group interest, antibigotry, mutual respect, and coalition building became the hallmark of "the new pluralism," a movement Levine is widely credited with launching. He has published several dozen articles on ethnicity and pluralism, and ten recent books carry chapters he has authored.

STANFORD M. LYMAN is currently the Robert J. Morrow Eminent Scholar and professor of social science at Florida Atlantic University, Boca Raton, Florida. Lyman has published widely in the area of sociology and is the author of seventeen books, among which are: *Chinese Americans* (1974), *The Asian in the West* (1970), *The Asian in North America* (1977), and *Chinatown and Little Tokyo* (1986). He has also authored *The Black American in Sociological Thought* (1972) and three works on phenomenological sociological theory with Marvin B. Scott: *A Sociology of the Absurd* (1989), *The Revolt of the Students* (1970), and *The Drama of Social Reality* (1975). His most recent books, coauthored with Arthur J. Vidich, are titled, *American Sociology: Worldly Rejections of Religion and Their Directions* (1985) and *Social Order and the Public Philosophy: An Analysis and Interpretation of the Work of Herbert Blumer* (1988). Forthcoming is *Civilization: Contents, Discontents, Malcontents and Other Essays in Social Theory*.

WORNIE L. REED is currently chairperson of the Black Studies Department and director of the William Monroe Trotter Institute for the Study of Black Culture at the University of Massachusetts at Boston. Prior to that position, he was a member of the Department of Sociology and an associate in the Division of Health Care Research in the School of Medicine at Washington University. He received his B.S. degree at Alabama State University and M.S. and Ph.D. degrees in sociology from Boston University. His background includes positions in the federal government and private industry as well as higher education. In January 1990, Reed assumed the presidency of the National Congress of Black Faculty.

CLARA E. RODRIGUEZ is associate professor of sociology at Fordham University, where she had formerly been dean. A visiting scholar in 1988 at the Massachusetts Institute of Technology, she is the author of numerous articles on Puerto Ricans in the United States and is a recognized authority on the subject. Her most recent book is *Puerto Ricans: Born in the U.S.A.* (1989). She is currently working on research supported by the Rockefeller Foundation.

PETER I. ROSE is Sophia Smith Professor and director of the American Studies Diploma Program at Smith College, where he was chair of the department of sociology and anthropology from 1967 to 1974 and 1979 to 1980. He is also a member of the graduate faculty of the University of Massachusetts. He has been a visiting professor at Clark College, University of Colorado, Wesleyan, Yale, and Harvard; senior Fulbright lecturer in England, Japan, and Australia; visiting scholar at Harvard and the Chinese Academy of Social Sciences in Beijing; Oldendorff lecturer in Tilburg, The Netherlands; resident scholar in Bellagio, Italy; and, most recently, visiting senior fellow, refugee studies programmer at Oxford University. President-elect of the Eastern Sociological Society for 1991–1992, Rose is author of *They and We* (4th ed., 1990), *The Subject Is Race* (1967), *Strangers in Their Midst* (1977), and *Mainstream and Margins* (1983) and is co-author of *Sociology* (2d ed., 1982), and *Over Vreemdeling en Vluchteling (On Strangers and Refugees)* (1983).

C. MATTHEW SNIPP is an associate professor of rural sociology and sociology at the University of Wisconsin–Madison. He received his Ph.D. in sociology in 1981 from the University of Wisconsin. He has been a research fellow at the U.S. Bureau of the Census, and he is currently a fellow at the Center for Advanced Study in the Behavioral Sciences. Snipp has published numerous works on the demography, economic development, poverty, and unemployment of American Indians. His most recent book is titled *American Indians: The First of This Land*. In collaboration with Gene F. Summers, Snipp's current research and writing deals with poverty and unemployment on American Indian reservations.

GENE F. SUMMERS received his Ph.D. in 1962 from the University of Tennessee where he was an NDEA fellow. He also was an NIMH postdoctoral fellow at the University of Wisconsin in 1964–1965 and a Fulbright Senior Research Fellow to the University of Bergen (Norway) in 1978. He also has been a distinguished visiting scholar at the University of South Florida and Guelph University (Canada). He currently is professor and chair of rural sociology at the University of Wisconsin. In addition to monographs and journal articles, his major publications include *Attitude Measurement* (1970), *Industrial Invasion of Nonmetropolitan America* (1975), *Nonmetropolitan Industrial Growth and Community Change* (1979), and *Technology and Social Change in Rural Areas* (1983).